Vergil's
AENEID

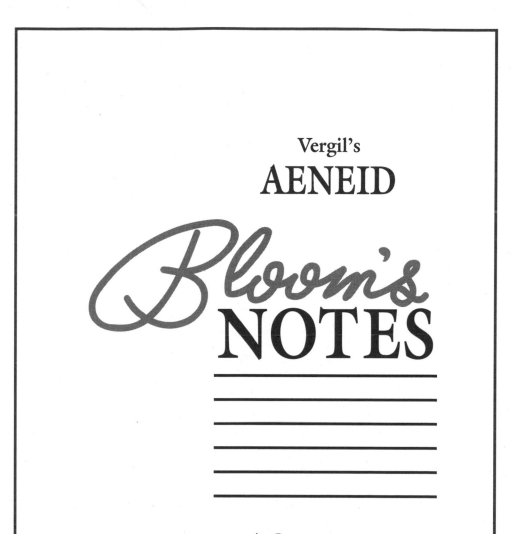

NOTES

A Contemporary
Literary Views Book

Edited and with an Introduction by
HAROLD BLOOM

First Printing
1 3 5 7 9 8 6 4 2

Cover Illustration: - The Vatican Museums

Library of Congress Cataloging-in-Publication Data

Vergil's Aeneid / edited and with an introduction by Harold Bloom.
p. cm. – (Bloom's Notes)
Includes bibliographical references (p.) and index.
Summary: Includes a brief biography of the author, thematic and structural analysis of the work, critical views, and an index of themes and ideas.
ISBN 0-7910-4051-8. — ISBN 0-7910-4079-8 (pbk.)
1. Virgil. Aeneis. 2. Aeneas (Legendary character) in literature. 3. Epic poetry, Latin – History and criticism. 4. Rome – In literature. [1. Virgil. Aeneis. 2. Epic poetry, Latin – History and criticism.] I. Bloom, Harold. II. Series.
PA6825.V5   1995
873'.01 – dc20
95-45112
CIP
AC

Chelsea House Publishers
1974 Sproul Road, Suite 400
P.O. Box 914
Broomall, PA 19008-0914

Contents

User's Guide

This volume is designed to present biographical, critical, and bibliographical information on Vergil and the *Aeneid.* Following Harold Bloom's introduction, there appears a detailed biography of the author, discussing the major events in his life and his important literary works. Then follows a thematic and structural analysis of the work, in which significant themes, patterns, and motifs are traced. An annotated list of characters supplies brief information on the chief characters in the work.

A selection of critical extracts, derived from previously published material by leading critics, then follows. The extracts consist of such things as statements by the author on his work, early notices of the work, and later evaluations down to the present day. The items are arranged chronologically by date of first publication. A bibliography of Vergil's writings (including Latin texts as well as English translations), a list of additional books and articles on him and on the *Aeneid,* and an index of themes and ideas conclude the volume.

Harold Bloom is Sterling Professor of the Humanities at Yale University and Henry W. and Albert A. Berg Professor of English at the New York University Graduate School. He is the author of twenty books and the editor of more than thirty anthologies of literature and literary criticism.

Professor Bloom's works include *Shelley's Mythmaking* (1959), *The Visionary Company* (1961), *Blake's Apocalypse* (1963), *Yeats* (1970), *A Map of Misreading* (1975), *Kabbalah and Criticism* (1975), and *Agon: Towards a Theory of Revisionism* (1982). *The Anxiety of Influence* (1973) sets forth Professor Bloom's provocative theory of the literary relationships between the great writers and their predecessors. His most recent books are *The American Religion* (1992) and *The Western Canon* (1994).

Professor Bloom earned his Ph.D. from Yale University in 1955 and has served on the Yale faculty since then. He is a 1985 MacArthur Foundation Award recipient and served as the Charles Eliot Norton Professor of Poetry at Harvard University in 1987–88. He is currently the editor of the Chelsea House series Major Literary Characters and Modern Critical Views, and other Chelsea House series in literary criticism.

Introduction

HAROLD BLOOM

W. R. Johnson, one of Vergil's most acute critics, submits that the poet of the *Aeneid* persuades us of his compassion for others by "the nakedness, the purity of his initial pity for himself." Johnson strongly reminds us that Vergil was an Epicurean both by temperament and by spiritual and philosophical conviction. Epicurus and his Roman disciple, the poet Lucretius, saw the human being as too flawed to will either personal happiness or a just political order. The Epicurean-Lucretian elitism preaches release from ignorance as the only salvation for a rational few; empire cannot save anyone, for it is founded upon the illusion of civic virtue. Going within the self is the Epicurean path to the only truth that matters: personal, individual, disillusioned, denying transcendence. The two dominant poetic influences upon Vergil were Homer and Lucretius; the spiritual influence that mattered was wholly Epicurean. Nothing could have been more mistaken than the Christian misreading of Vergil, which Dante made permanent among us. Vergil has no hope, and his only belief is the faithless faith of the Epicureans, who accepted human suffering as inevitable, except for that rational remnant that could abandon all illusion.

Vergil's greatest originality, which redeems the *Aeneid* from its confusions, is his powerfully negative imagination. The one figure who does not embody all of this imagination is Aeneas, whom many readers will regard as a prig or a stick, who comes to life only when he is being a cad in regard to Dido or a brute in regard to Turnus. It cannot be said that Aeneas always shares his creator's extraordinary sensitivity to suffering and to pain. True to his undoubted model, Vergil's patron the emperor Augustus, Aeneas keeps his mind upon the foundation of Rome and its future greatness. Since Aeneas is anything but an Epicurean hero (if there could be such an oddity), we have the puzzle, as we read the *Aeneid,* as to whether we are to trust the song or the singer. The singer, despite his Augustan allegiances, maintains a powerful and desperate undersong that is at variance with the poem's overt and official purposes. Who after all is the Muse of the *Aeneid?* Lucretius celebrated an Epicurean Venus, but Vergil's poem is dominated by the sinister queen of Heaven, the vindictive Juno, who wishes to destroy Aeneas, the rather unlikely son of Venus. Juno is a great nightmare, inspirited by the full vivacity of Vergil's negative imagination, including doubtless his fear of women. Her stormy wrath makes her the Goddess of Resentment, an inward brooder whose inflamed heart memorializes every possible grudge. Poor Dido, when abandoned, becomes the authentic high priestess of Juno, particularly by the act of self-immolation.

Since Aeneas eventually triumphs, Juno presumably does not, but actually she does, since her compact with Jupiter rather subtly involves his taking on much of her dark spirit, once she has given in. What are we to make of Vergil's Jupiter, who is anything but an Epicurean god? The gods of Epicurus and of Lucretius serenely dwell apart, being sublimely indifferent to human fate. Vergil is celebrated for always seeing two sides to everything, but Jupiter is simply not that dialectical. It is because of Jupiter that the poem's two most attractive persons are destroyed so dreadfully, punished for being so full of life. Dido and Turnus only can be themselves, which for Jupiter is unforgivable. Aeneas the exile, pious but drab when compared to Turnus and to Dido, is therefore acceptable to the high god. Either there is a Vergilian irony in this, or more likely it is the revenge of the poet's Epicureanism upon his patriotic Augustanism. Aeneas wins, but at the cost of an extraordinary self-abnegation.

Vergil weeps not so much the tears of a universal nature but of a poetry that must reconcile itself to the power and purposes of the state. Dying at fifty-one, Vergil requested that the *Aeneid* be burned rather than published, a plea that Augustus refused. The supposed reason for Vergil's Dido-like desire was that the poem had not been completed. Perhaps there were other sentiments that also governed the dying Vergil. He cannot have been altogether happy with his poem's overt celebration of empire and order. The elegiac voice, as Adam Parry demonstrated, is always the undersong in this Augustan epic. Aeneas is a strange hero since, as Parry observes, he serves a purely impersonal power. Finally the *Aeneid* seems the most elegiac of epics, and yet Epicurus refused to grant any significance to human suffering. If we care for Aeneas at all, it is because of the quality of his grief, his perpetual suffering as he remembers the fall of Troy. Vergil's *Aeneid* achieves greatness because it is a great poem of defeat, but also of the heroism (if it is that) of sustaining defeat. Divided in his own deepest self, Vergil may have doubted whether his poem deserved to survive. Posterity would appear to have resolved any such doubt. ✤

Biography of Vergil

Publius Vergilius Maro (whose name has traditionally been Anglicized as Virgil, although Vergil is now the preferred spelling among classical scholars) was born on October 15, 70 B.C.E., at Andes, a village near the town of Mantua, Italy. Vergil's father was a poor potter, but he married the daughter of a wealthy landowner and was thereby able to give his son a good education. After being instructed at his father's farm and villa in Mantua, Vergil went to Cremona and then to Rome for higher education. At this time he became acquainted with the circle of writers centering around the poet Catullus, thereby becoming imbued with Alexandrian ideals of poetry, which stressed delicacy and complexity of diction and extreme refinement in poetic sensibility.

Vergil's early manhood coincided with the most turbulent period in the history of the Roman republic. Julius Caesar's invasion of Rome in 49 B.C.E., in defiance of the Senate's order to lay down his arms, inaugurated nearly twenty years of civil war. Vergil retreated to Naples, in the south of Italy, where he studied with the Epicurean philosopher Siro, whose villa Vergil apparently inherited sometime prior to 41 B.C.E. Caesar's murder in 44 led to a power struggle between Octavius Caesar, Mark Antony, and M. Lepidus. Octavius ultimately prevailed, and a distribution of land to war veterans in 41 resulted in the appropriation of the estate of Vergil's father. Only through the intervention of Vergil's friend C. Asinius Pollio was Vergil's own land saved from confiscation.

Vergil had begun his first work, the *Eclogues,* around 45 and completed them no later than 37. This group of ten short poems are idealized descriptions of pastoral life (they are sometimes referred to as pastorals or bucolics) modeled upon the works of the Greek poet Theocritus. The fourth eclogue predicts the birth of a child who will usher in a golden age; many commentators in the Middle Ages believed this to be a prediction of the birth of Jesus Christ, but the reference is probably to a child of Pollio, who had encouraged Vergil to write the poems, or some other political figure of the time. These poems are written in the Alexandrian manner and designed for a small coterie of educated readers, but they proved popular and some were adapted as mimes.

Around 41 Vergil had struck up a friendship with the poet Quintus Horatius Flaccus (Horace), and upon the publication of the *Eclogues* both poets came under the influence of Octavius Caesar and the celebrated artistic patron C. Maecenas. The fifth poem in Horace's first book of satires (dated to 37) records a trip he took with Vergil and others to Brundisium (Brindisi).

Vergil spent seven years working on the *Georgics,* a collection of four long poems whose surface theme is agricultural life, but which also deal exhaustively with philosophical, political, and artistic issues. The work was probably completed by 30, and each of the four poems contains an address to Maecenas.

In antiquity it was believed that Vergil spent eleven years (29–19) working on the *Aeneid,* but we first hear of the work only around 26, when the poet Propertius mentions the commencement of a work that would prove greater than Homer's *Iliad.* This epic poem in twelve books is certainly the greatest work of its kind in Latin literature. Although clearly influenced by the epics of Homer (as well as by the *Annales* of Quintus Ennius, written in the late second century B.C.E., and the philosophical poem *De Rerum Natura* by T. Lucretius Carus, written in the middle of the first century B.C.E.), the *Aeneid* is a powerful and distinctive narrative of the founding of Roman civilization by Aeneas, a Trojan soldier who is said to have survived the defeat of Troy by the Greeks and founded a new colony in Italy.

Around 19 Vergil left Italy to travel in Greece and the Near East in order to complete the polishing of the *Aeneid.* He met Octavius (who, after his defeat of his rivals in 31 at the Battle of Actium, had declared himself emperor and changed his name to Augustus) in Athens and was persuaded by him to return to Rome. He fell ill in Megara, Greece, and died on September 20, 19 B.C.E., in Brundisium. The *Aeneid* never received Vergil's final polishing, as some lines throughout the poem are incomplete. Vergil had, indeed, instructed his literary executor,

Alfenus Varius, to burn the *Aeneid* if he left it unfinished, but Augustus ordered the poem to be published.

A group of nineteen poems, some of them of considerable length, were believed in antiquity to be written by Vergil in his youth; but modern scholars doubt the authenticity of nearly all of them. These poems (which include the *Catalepton, Culex, Ciris, Copa, Moretum,* and *Aetna*) are now generally published collectively as the *Appendix Vergiliana.*

The *Aeneid* was praised throughout antiquity and was widely used as a school textbook; but other critics claimed to find many borrowings from other poets, both Latin and Greek. The scholar Servius compiled an extensive commentary on all three of Vergil's works in the late fourth or early fifth century C.E.; this commentary appears to incorporate the work of an earlier scholar, Aelius Donatus. In modern times commentaries on the *Aeneid* have been written by Otto Ribbeck (1859–68), John Conington (1858–71), and R. D. Williams (1972–73).

The figure of Vergil himself became a revered one in antiquity and the Middle Ages. Possibly as early as the second century C.E., a procedure known as the *Sortes Vergilianae* came into being, involving the random opening of the *Aeneid* for purposes of fortune-telling. Vergil was regarded as a poet who anticipated the teachings of Jesus Christ, and in this capacity he was used as a character in Dante's *Inferno.*

The *Aeneid* has attracted the skills of many translators. In 1553 the Scottish poet Gawin Douglas published a translation in Scots verse. John Dryden translated the whole of Vergil into English in 1697, and his translation established the heroic couplet as the standard meter for English epic poetry. Such noted poets as William Morris (1876), C. Day Lewis (1952), and Robert Fitzgerald (1983) have also produced distinguished translations. ❖

Thematic and Structural Analysis

Arma, or weapons, is the first word of the *Aeneid,* and indeed the epic springs from war. At the root of the story is the legendary Trojan War (which may have taken place around 1200 B.C.E.), in which the Trojans were besieged and after ten years beaten by the Greeks for their part in Helen's abduction; according to legend, the Trojan hero Aeneas then journeyed from his ruined city to find a new home, eventually settling in Italy and founding the Roman people. Between the semi-mythical Trojan War and the time Vergil wrote his epic, more than a thousand years had passed, in which a village called Rome was indeed settled and gradually grew to rule the Mediterranean. The Romans achieved this through centuries of warfare, defeating the other tribes of Italy, the Carthaginians of North Africa, and the Greeks, until finally the Roman Empire, stretching from Syria to Spain, was established by Augustus after he conquered his internal enemies through a bloody civil war that ended in 31 B.C.E.

It was in the new, peaceful Augustan era that Vergil began his epic poem, and part of his object was to celebrate the spread of Roman rule and the national character that had achieved it. Focusing on the figure of Aeneas, Vergil interwove Roman history and Greek and Italian myth to reconstruct a fabulous past for his people. In part he modeled his project on the great Homeric epics of the eighth century B.C.E., the *Iliad* and the *Odyssey,* the former describing the Trojan War and the latter portraying the Greek hero Odysseus' return home from that war. For this may have been Vergil's second object: to create for the Romans a literary text as powerful as these of the Greeks—a people the Romans had conquered but whose seemingly superior culture they had always envied. Yet although Vergil clearly modeled many of his poem's episodes, characters, and constructions upon the Greek works, his text forms a painstakingly original portrait of the Roman character, embodied in the hero, Aeneas, as he struggles from the ruins of Troy to found the Roman people.

Book one opens at the heart of the struggle: Having fled Troy, Aeneas has been voyaging for seven years to find a new home for his people and gods—a home fated to rule the Mediterranean—but he is vindictively thwarted by Juno, queen of the gods, who has always hated the Trojans and wants her beloved Carthaginians to rule the Mediterranean. She has obstructed Aeneas' path ever since he sailed from Troy, and now she bids the wind god, Aeolus, to create a storm that will destroy Aeneas' fleet.

We first see Aeneas groaning as his ships are scattered and lost in the tumultuous sea. This initial impression of the hero— a man battered but honorable, longing to save his people— persists throughout the epic, as does the epithet often attached to his name: *pius,* or dutiful. Neptune, the god of the sea, quells the storm, however, and Aeneas lands at Libya with just seven of his twenty ships left. He encourages his people to have hope, although he himself, "burdened and sick at heart, [feigns] hope in his look." This stoicism is typical of Vergil's hero, and indeed of the Roman concept of virtue.

It may seem that Aeneas, though virtuous, is helpless, but we now meet an important ally: Venus, the goddess of love, who is in fact his mother. She is a formidable counterpart to Juno and, upset to see her son stranded far from Italy, approaches the king of gods, Jupiter, and reminds him of Aeneas' destiny. But to travel on to Italy Aeneas will need help, so Jupiter agrees to make the local queen, Dido, friendly to the fugitives. Dido herself fled to Libya from her brother, who had killed her husband, and she has reason to fear strangers. With the gods' intervention, though, and her own natural empathy for the Trojans' struggles, the beautiful, judicious queen graciously welcomes Aeneas, promises aid, and invites the Trojans to a feast.

Venus, however, decides to ensure her son's kindly treatment by plotting to have Dido—faithful to her dead husband's memory—fall in love with Aeneas. To accomplish this, Venus has her divine son, Amor, temporarily take the place of Aeneas' son, Ascanius, and fill the queen with love. At the banquet, the disguised godling gradually makes the memory of Dido's husband fade, as a "living love" awakens. Before the night is over

Dido has drunk "long draughts of love" and implores Aeneas to tell his story.

Although "shudder[ing] at the memory and shrink[ing] again in grief," Aeneas tells of his terrible adventures before reaching Carthage (**books two and three**). He begins with the end of the Trojan War, when the Trojans find the famous wooden horse on their shores and imagine it means that the Greeks have retreated. The priest Laocoön does not believe this, however: "Even when Greeks bring gifts," he says, "I fear them, gifts and all." But his kinsmen think his fears are unfounded; they are easily convinced by the Greek "refugee," Sinon, who claims that the horse is in fact sacred, and persuades them to take it into the city. Laocoön's mistrust is then seen to be punished when out of the sea swim two monstrous serpents who twine themselves about him and his sons. (This scene, with its intense, highly colored quality, is typical of Vergil's vision, as are his many detailed naturalistic descriptions.) Terrified by this portent, the Trojans drag the horse into the city, and that night, as they sleep, Sinon opens the horse to release its cargo of Greek soldiers.

While Aeneas sleeps, the dead Trojan hero Hector appears to him in a dream, tells him that Troy is ruined, and bids him to flee the city with its household gods and "find for them the great walls" of their new home, Rome. But Aeneas, waking to find his city in flames, decides to die fighting and, gathering a small troop of men, plunges into the chaotic city. But the Trojans have no chance: Greeks are everywhere, even inside the palace of the aged Trojan king, Priam. Aeneas watches helplessly as Priam tries to fight off the invading Greeks until his wife, Hecuba, pulls him to her side on the household altar where she and her daughters, "like white doves blown down in a black storm, [cling] together, enfolding holy images in their arms." One of the old couple's few remaining sons is chopped down as he runs toward them; then Priam himself is murdered upon the altar.

Aeneas, witnessing this horrific scene, thinks suddenly of his own father, son, and wife. But before he can return to them he sees, hiding in a corner, Helen—the reputed cause of the entire war. He cannot bear to imagine her returning like a queen to

Greece when all the Trojan women will become slaves of Greeks, and he prepares to kill her—but at this moment Venus appears and tells him that it is not Helen but the will of the gods that "brings Troy from her height into the dust." She strips the veil from her son's mortal eyes and allows him to see the gods themselves tearing down the city's walls, in another of Vergil's intensely visual scenes.

Now Aeneas has no choice but to accept his city's downfall. With Venus' protection, he returns home, but his frightened family cannot agree to leave until a portent occurs: Suddenly the head of Aeneas' son, Ascanius, is ringed by harmless flames. This portent is followed by others, all pointing to the promise of a future elsewhere.

The family sets out—Aeneas carrying his father, Anchises, upon his back and holding his son's hand, with his wife, Creusa, behind. They proceed in terror through the burning city and the plundering Greeks, but in a moment of panic Creusa is lost. Leaving the others in safety, Aeneas returns to search for his wife, crying her name frantically in the darkness. But only her ghost appears to tell him he must leave. Weeping, he tries to embrace her, in a classical motif of agonizing futility:

> Three times
> I tried to put my arms around her neck,
> Three times enfolded nothing, as the wraith
> Slipped through my fingers, bodiless as wind,
> Or like a flitting dream.

Sadly Aeneas returns to his father and son, but finds with them now a large company of exiles, ready for "whatever lands [he would] lead them to by sea."

In **book three** Aeneas continues his story for Dido, recounting now his people's travels before reaching Carthage. At their first stop, Thrace, Aeneas hopes to establish the new city, but when he plucks twigs to construct an altar, "dark blood [drips] down to soak and foul the soil." Quickly setting sail from that "earth stained with blood"—earth that may recall Vergil's own Italy during the bloody civil wars—the Trojans then learn through prophecy that they must reach "the self-same land that bore" them. This seeming to be Crete, they optimistically establish a new town there, planting fields and returning to life. But this attempt too is soon destroyed when plague strikes. At last they learn that they must strive for Italy. But with Juno's hostility this is not so easy. Among the various stops on the Trojans' troubled route west are the Strophades, where a desperately longed-for meal is befouled by the resident Harpies, "flying things with young girls' faces, but foul ooze below, talons for hands, pale famished nightmare mouths."

Growing increasingly desperate, Aeneas and his followers reach a part of Greece ruled by one of Priam's sons, Helenus. A prophet, Helenus tells Aeneas of his subsequent travels and that he will know he has reached the appointed land when he sees a white sow suckling thirty young. The Trojans carefully follow Helenus' counsel, avoiding Italy's western coast, staying clear of the whirlpool Charybdis and monster Scylla. They land, however, on the island of the man-eating Cyclops but are warned away by a terrified Greek who was left behind by Odysseus when he made his own difficult journey home from the Trojan War. Thankful for the warning, Aeneas takes the frightened man on board, and they quickly leave. (This scene is an example of Vergil's inventive use of his model for the first half of the epic, the *Odyssey*. Instead of having Aeneas experience just what Odysseus had on the Cyclops' island—the monster's man-eating anger—Vergil has Aeneas experience Odysseus' disregard for one of his own men. Vergil's story therefore offers a portrait of the Roman character that compares favorably to that of the Greek.)

At this point Aeneas' story is drawing to a close. All that remains is the sad epilogue: His father Anchises, "solace in all affliction and mischance," dies just before Aeneas and his people reach Carthage. On this final note Aeneas falls silent.

By now (**book four**), Dido is hopelessly in love with the Trojan hero, "a wound of inward fire eating her away." Having sworn faithfulness to her dead husband, however, she goes to her sister, Anna, for advice. Anna persuades Dido that it would be good not only for her but for the Carthaginians to form a union with the Trojan hero, as they are surrounded in Libya by hostile peoples. She counsels Dido to contrive delays in order to keep the Trojans there.

In her tormented passion Dido neglects her city: "Towers, half-built, [rise] no farther; men no longer [train] in arms or [toil] to make harbors and battlements impregnable." Dido thus abandons the very object for which Aeneas strives—the construction of a powerful city; to a Roman this civic irresponsibility would be a great moral weakness. Juno, observing this threat to her goal of making Carthage the chief Mediterranean power, quickly proposes to Venus that both their ends be served by having Dido and Aeneas marry—thereby keeping Aeneas safe, but away from his destined Rome forever. Venus pretends to go along with the plan. The impression Roman readers would have of Dido's moral weakness would be furthered, however, in the "marriage" that Juno arranges. For it occurs in secrecy, while Dido and Aeneas are hunting. Juno concocts a thunderstorm, the pair rush for cover into a cave, and there they consummate their passion—but, ominously, only Dido "[calls] it marriage."

Word of their union quickly spreads through Rumor, one of Vergil's most striking personifications, and Jupiter sends the messenger, Mercury, to Aeneas to chide him for lingering in Carthage. Aeneas, shaken by the divine message, burns "to leave that land of the sweet life behind"—and here Vergil is evoking in his audience's minds the image of Augustus' enemy in the recent civil wars, Marc Antony, who forsook Rome for the Eqyptian queen Cleopatra.

But leaving Dido is not so easy, and her desperate struggles first to keep Aeneas and then to control her own passions form perhaps the epic's most dramatic and poignant sections. The queen moves through stages of rationality, rage, and mourning but is not able to keep Aeneas, who pleads that he is compelled by duty and also claims that the "marriage" in fact was not legitimate. Like the wax that kept Odysseus' men safe near the entrancing and deadly Sirens, "God's will [blocks] the man's once kindly ears." Aeneas is resolved to fulfill his mission, and so Dido resolves to die. She stabs herself with Aeneas' sword as his ships leave her harbor—but not before cursing the future Romans with the enmity of Carthage, which

Vergil's readers would recognize well in the Carthaginian wars of the previous centuries.

Book five offers relief to these dramatic events. Aeneas and his company, unaware of the tragedy they have left behind, land again in Sicily, where Anchises had died. It is now a year since then and time for Aeneas to hold anniversary rituals and games in his father's memory. His men and some of those of Acestes (the Trojan-blooded ruler there) compete in ship and foot races, javelin and archery contests, and wrestling. The events provide some comedy—as when the overly cautious helmsman Menoetes is thrown into the sea by his too-eager captain, Gyas, in the ship race—and are marked by portents: A brilliant but harmless snake appears at Anchises' tomb; an arrow shot in the archery contest bursts into flames. This book also notes the beginning of the historical cataloging frequent in later sections, where Vergil presents his characters as ancestors of prominent Romans of his own times. But the celebrations are marred by several events: Juno impels the travel-weary Trojan women to set fire to the ships; Anchises' ghost appears before Aeneas to tell him he must travel to the underworld before reaching his destination; and, once Aeneas has allowed those who are weary to remain with Acestes while he and the others sail on, his diligent helmsman, Palinurus, is tricked by Sleep and tumbles into the sea.

The ships continue their course, however, and in **book six** the Trojans at last land in Italy, at Cumae. Here Aeneas follows Helenus' earlier instructions and finds the Sibyl, the priestess of Diana and Apollo, who tells him of the conflicts he must still face in Italy, and of how he may first reach the underworld.

The necessary tasks performed (the most famous being plucking the golden bough from deep in a dark forest), Aeneas and the Sibyl enter the cavern that leads to the underworld. They pass hosts of bodiless monsters and crowds of souls clamoring to cross the waters of Cocytus and Acheron into the underworld proper; there the ferryman, Charon, allows Aeneas and the Sibyl to cross once he has seen the golden bough. On the other side they reach the Stygian swamps, region of infants and suicides; among them is the soul of Dido, who refuses to listen to Aeneas. The Sibyl urges him through the souls of warriors, past the road to dreadful Tartarus, where the souls of criminals and sinners are endlessly tortured, and finally into Elysium, the Blessed Groves.

Here are the heroes, the chaste, the beneficent thinkers and creators; here are a whole new sun and stars. Aeneas finds his father in a lush green valley, where the two joyously meet. Then Anchises tells his son about the transmigration of souls: Once they are cleansed of their former fleshly contaminants, they enter new bodies. Before Anchises wait the souls of the entire line of future Roman heroes, from Aeneas' own future son to Augustus of Vergil's time. With this promise of a radiant future, Aeneas and the Sibyl slip through the gates of sleep into the upper world.

Proceeding smoothly on their journey, Aeneas and his company at last reach the western coast of Italy, where the Tiber spills into the sea (**book seven**). This region, the future site of Rome, is ruled by Latinus, whose daughter, Lavinia, is readying for marriage with the neighboring Italian king Turnus—despite the fact that the portents warn against this union, indicating instead "no Latin alliance" for Lavinia but marriage with a foreigner. When Aeneas' envoys meanwhile approach Latinus with the proposal that the Trojans settle peacefully nearby, fulfilling Aeneas' destiny, Latinus realizes that Aeneas must be "the man called for by fate" to wed his daughter, and welcomes them—breaking his daughter's engagement with Turnus.

It would seem that Aeneas has thus finally arrived—but Juno, always watching, resolves that if she cannot block Aeneas from founding Rome, she can make him pay for it, swearing that Lavinia's dowry will be bought with "blood, Trojan and Latin." Summoning from the underworld the hellish Fury Allecto, "her head alive and black with snakes," Juno bids her infect Latinus' wife, Amata, with a wild rage at the injustice of Turnus' broken engagement, throwing into chaos Latinus' own kingdom; Allecto then flies to Turnus and incites in him the urge to wage the "brute insanity of war" upon Latinus and the Trojans. Finally, the Fury stirs up violence between Latinus' people and the Trojans themselves by impelling Ascanius to shoot their sacred stag. Latinus is unable to keep his people from joining Turnus' war against the Trojans but will not open the official gates of war—so Juno does herself. The book concludes with a lengthy catalog of warriors, "as many as there are waves upon the sparkling sea," as Aeneas' new conflicts begin. The latter half of the epic is often referred to as the *Iliad* portion, for now Aeneas is faced with war, ostensibly over a woman.

As Aeneas, "heartsick at the woe of war," agonizes over this new situation, the god of the Tiber rises (**book eight**), assures him that where he has settled is the foretold site of the white suckling sow, and advises him to join forces with Latinus' enemies, the Arcadians, in fighting for his destined land and bride. The Arcadian king, Evander, is willing to join Aeneas and entertains him with tales of Hercules (another hero hated by Juno) and prophetic stories of the future Rome. He admits, however, that his own forces are slight, and so proposes that Aeneas solicit the aid of the Arcadians' allies, the Etruscans, who are eager to fight Turnus for harboring their exiled, monstrous king, Mezentius. But Evander gives his own son, Pallas—his "dear delight"—to Aeneas, to be trained by the great Trojan warrior.

As Aeneas completes his preparations for war among mortals, his mother does the same among the gods: She bids her husband, the smith-god Vulcan, to forge for her son a magnificent set of armor and weaponry. The resulting shield is a masterpiece, intricately adorned with images portraying the most dramatic moments of the future Rome. The centerpiece is the Battle of Actium, at which Augustus finally defeated Marc Antony and Cleopatra in 31 B.C.E., thus ending Rome's civil wars. Aeneas will therefore enter his own war shielded—in the eyes of his readers—with an image of a recent and horrifying war justly won.

The war itself (**books nine through twelve**) begins with the Trojans under a siege terribly like the one imposed upon them for ten years by the Greeks. And this fact reveals the high stakes of the war: Not only do the Trojans fight for their destined land; they fight for their very identity, having been devastated by the Greeks and now tauntingly called "twice-conquered" by the Italians.

Juno urges Turnus to launch the war before Aeneas has returned from soliciting aid, while his armies are barricaded in the camp. Like "a wolf on the prowl round a full sheepfold," Turnus tries to lure the Trojans and their allies out to fight by burning their ships (**book nine**). The ships, however, are transformed into sea nymphs—their bows "like a school of dolphins diving into the depths"—who later meet Aeneas returning from Tuscany by sea and urge him to hurry back to the battle. Before then, though, a pair of Trojan soldiers, Nisus and his young friend Euryalus, resolve to break through Turnus' siege to recall Aeneas. Stealing out at night like a pair of cats, they descend on the Italians, murdering many as they sleep. They hurry on their mission but are betrayed by Euryalus' plumed helmet as it glints in the moonlight. Both are killed, their heads impaled and displayed to the Trojans at dawn. The fighting begins in earnest then, but the Trojans, "trained in their long war," hold their walls—but not well enough to keep Turnus from infiltrating and slaughtering many before he escapes by leaping into the Tiber, where he floats "exultant to his fellow soldiers' hands."

Meanwhile, Venus and Juno argue bitterly over this violence, but because their cases are equal, Jupiter decides to let the battle continue equally (**book ten**). When Aeneas arrives with Pallas and the allied Arcadians and Etruscans, the battle rages. In the course of the spearing and cleaving, Pallas—Aeneas' protégé and charge—overeager at his first fight, attracts Turnus' attention. The much more powerful Turnus spears the boy through the chest and, unforgivably, to Aeneas, glories in his kill, tearing away Pallas' precious sword belt. Aeneas now rages "in fury wild as a torrent or a dark tornado" so that Juno, fearing for Turnus, removes him against his will from the battlefield. Aeneas instead vents his rage on Turnus' ally, the exiled Etruscan king Mezentius, killing first his son (whose filial piety in trying to defend his father moves Aeneas to pity), and then, unpityingly, Mezentius himself.

This initial carnage gives way to a respite: Both sides burn and bury their dead (**book eleven**), and Pallas is mournfully returned to his father. The Italians, meanwhile, grow doubtful of this war, but Turnus, still outraged at his betrayal, urges them on. As he rides out to lie in wait for Aeneas and his troops, the day's main fighting is carried on by others, the central figure being the Italian "hard-riding warrior queen," Camilla. Cherished since she was a child by the goddess Diana, Camilla and her cavalry are formidable and charge into the battle, slaughtering countless men. She is stalked, however, and eventually brought down by one man—who is in turn immediately killed by Diana's emissary, for daring "to pierce [Camilla's] body, impiously." The Trojans have many victories this day (indeed, Vergil seems often to sympathize with the Italians), but still Turnus and Aeneas have not met in battle.

This crucial meeting comes at last, when Turnus, his passion rising "hot and unquenchable," resolves to end the general warfare and instead fight Aeneas singly: "With our own blood let us two put an end to war," he says (**book twelve**). The two heroes prepare, and both sides, now under a peace pact, arrange themselves for the tremendous spectacle—but again Juno intervenes, encouraging Turnus' divine sister, Juturna, to save her brother. This Juturna does by goading an Italian to break the truce by hurling a spear across the line, so that again general warfare breaks out. Both Juno (through Juturna) and Venus take part now, the former always shielding Turnus and keeping him from the frustrated Aeneas, the latter magically healing her son when he is struck by an arrow. The two sides ravage each other, Aeneas and Turnus especially laying waste to all they encounter, "like snow-fed streams that foam and roar seaward down mountain-sides." But still the two heroes are unable to meet, until finally Turnus discovers and refuses his divine sister's protection. He calls Aeneas to single combat.

With all their armies and people watching in terror, Aeneas and Turnus at last meet, clashing like bulls. Turnus' sword, however, is shattered when it strikes Aeneas' divine armor, "snapped into fragments like an icicle." But still the immortals, unwilling to let the men fight on their own strength, intervene. The conflict seems doomed to eternal balance until finally Jove tells Juno that she and Juturna must yield. At last, resigned to fate, Juno does—but asks only that, after the Trojans have won, they not recreate Troy, but instead mingle with those they have conquered, allowing them to remain Italian. "Once and for all Troy fell," she says, "and with her name let her lie fallen."

Turnus' fate is now fixed. As Aeneas moves toward him with his spear, Turnus finds himself nightmarishly weak, unable to move. Aeneas sends his spear through Turnus' thigh, and the Italian hero crumples. But as the Trojan stands over him with his sword, Turnus asks for mercy. Aeneas, so often pensive and pitying, is about to relent—until he catches sight of the sword belt that Turnus had torn from Pallas' body. Enraged, crying that this is just retribution, Aeneas plunges his blade into Turnus' chest—and the Trojans, at last, are the victors. ✤

—*Jane Shumate*
Bryn Mawr College

(All above translations are Robert Fitzgerald's.)

List of Characters

Juno is the queen of the gods and wife of Jupiter. Her vendetta against Aeneas provides the epic's chief conflict, first preventing the Trojans from reaching Italy, then embroiling them in war once they arrive.

Aeneas, the hero of the epic, leads a group of refugees from Troy over the Mediterranean to a new home, destined to be Rome. Imbued with classical Roman traits of endurance, dutifulness, discipline, and physical strength, he is also modeled by Vergil to have sensitivity and pathos.

Neptune is the god of the sea, often powerful and violent, but here portrayed as gentle and righteous when he quells a sea storm.

Achates is Aeneas' faithful companion.

Acestes is a king of Sicily who is kind to the Trojans.

Jupiter is king of the gods and husband of Juno, often mediating between her and Venus as he oversees Aeneas' progress.

Venus, goddess of love and sensuality, is Aeneas' mother and crucial ally in his quest for Rome. She often undermines Juno's destructive plots and appears magically to save or protect her son, concealing him in mist, for example, or healing his wounds.

Dido, queen of Carthage, is induced by Venus to fall in love with Aeneas. When he leaves her to resume his journey, her humiliation and agony drive her to suicide.

Anchises is Aeneas' old father, once the chosen lover of Venus, for which he paid by becoming lame. He accompanies Aeneas and the other fugitives but dies in Sicily.

Ascanius, or Iulus, is Aeneas' son, who accompanies his father to Italy and matures throughout the epic to become a young soldier.

Amor, Venus' divine son, assumes Ascanius' identity in order to infuse Dido with love for Aeneas.

Laocoön is a Trojan priest who warns, correctly, that the wooden horse left behind by the Greeks is dangerous. He and his sons are destroyed by a deadly pair of sea serpents.

Sinon is a Greek who pretends to be abandoned by his comrades and who then convinces the Trojans to take the wooden horse within their walls.

Priam is the aged king of the Trojans who witnesses the end of his city and people and is murdered upon his own altar.

Hector, one of Priam and Hecuba's sons, a Trojan hero killed in the war, appears to Aeneas in a dream and bids him leave the ruined city.

Hecuba, queen of Troy, witnesses the destruction of her people.

Creusa is Aeneas' Trojan wife, who is lost as the family tries to leave the burning city. She appears to Aeneas as a ghost and urges him to flee.

Palinurus, Aeneas' helmsman, is tricked by Sleep and killed.

Apollo is the god of the sun, rationality, prophecy, and healing.

Helenus, a prophet and son of Priam, is a king of Epirus.

Anna, Dido's sister, encourages the queen's passion for Aeneas.

Sibyl is a priestess of Apollo and Diana who leads Aeneas into the underworld.

Diana is the goddess of hunting, wilderness, and the moon.

Charon is the ferryman of the underworld.

Latinus, a king of central Italy, welcomes Aeneas as ally and bridegroom and so incurs the wrath and war of Turnus.

Lavinia is Latinus and Amata's daughter, betrothed to Turnus.

Turnus, a king of Italy, wages war upon the Trojans and their allies when his engagement to Lavinia is broken. He is portrayed sympathetically, and his death concludes the epic.

Amata, the mother of Lavinia and wife of Latinus, helps provoke the war between Italians and Trojans through her allegiance to Turnus.

Allecto is a Fury who incites the war between Italians and Trojans.

Evander, king of Arcadia in Italy, befriends the Trojans and offers them his aid and his adored son, Pallas, in their war against the Italians.

Pallas, Evander's son, is killed by Turnus. His precious sword belt, taken as a prize by Turnus, is instrumental in the epic's last act.

Mezentius, king of the Etruscans but exiled by them for his monstrous cruelties, is an ally of Turnus and is killed by Aeneas.

Vulcan, god of fire and metalwork and husband of Venus, crafts Aeneas' armor.

Nisus, a Trojan and a beloved friend of Euryalus, attempts a brave mission but is killed.

Euryalus, a young Trojan beloved by Nisus, is killed with him while attempting a daring mission.

Camilla is an Italian warrior beloved by Diana. She fights fiercely for Turnus but is killed.

Juturna, the divine sister of Turnus, attempts to save him from his fate at Aeneas' hands. ✤

Critical Views

[John Dryden (1631–1700), aside from being the leading British poet and playwright of his age, was also a pioneering critic. His chief critical work is *Of Dramatick Poesy* (1668), but valuable critical utterances are also found in the prefaces and dedications to various works. In the following extract from the dedication to his translation of the *Aeneid* (1697), Dryden believes that Vergil's fundamental message in his epic was obedience to authority, a message instilled in him by the chaos of the civil wars at the end of the Roman republic.]

I say that *Virgil* having maturely weigh'd the Condition of the Times in which he liv'd: that an entire Liberty was not to be retriev'd: that the present Settlement had the prospect of a long continuance in the same Family, or those adopted into it: that he held his Paternal Estate from the Bounty of the Conqueror, by whom he was likewise enrich'd, esteem'd and cherish'd: that this Conquerour, though of a bad kind, was the very best of it: that the Arts of Peace flourish'd under him: that all Men might be happy if they would be quiet: that now he was in possession of the whole, yet he shar'd a great part of his Authority with the Senate: That he would be chosen into the Ancient Offices of the Commonwealth, and Rul'd by the Power which he deriv'd from them; and Prorogu'd his Government from time to time: Still, as it were, threatning to dismiss himself from Publick Cares, which he exercis'd more for the common Good, than for any delight he took in greatness: These things, I say, being consider'd by the Poet, he concluded it to be the Interest of his Country to be so Govern'd: To infuse an awful Respect into the People, towards such a Prince: By that respect to confirm their Obedience to him; and by that Obedience to make them Happy. This was the Moral of his Divine Poem: Honest in the Poet: Honourable to the Emperour, whom he derives from a Divine Extraction; and reflecting part of that Honour on the *Roman* People, whom he derives also from the *Trojans;* and not only profitable, but necessary to the present Age; and likely to be such to their Posterity. That it was the receiv'd Opinion, that the *Romans* were descended from the *Trojans*, and *Julius Cæsar* from *Iulus* the Son of *Æneas*, was enough for *Virgil*; tho' perhaps he thought not so himself: Or that *Æneas* ever was in *Italy*, which *Bochartus* manifestly proves. And *Homer*, where he says that *Jupiter* hated the House of *Priam*, and was resolv'd to transfer the Kingdom to the Family of *Æneas*, yet mentions nothing of his leading a Colony into a Foreign Country, and setling there. But that the *Romans* valued themselves on their *Trojan* Ancestry, is so undoubted a Truth, that I need not prove it. Even the Seals which we have remaining of *Julius Cæsar*, which we know to be Antique, have the Star of *Venus* over them, though they were all graven after his Death, as a Note that he was Deifi'd. I doubt not but one Reason, why *Augustus* should be so passionately concern'd for the preservation of the *Æneis*, which its Author had Condemn'd to be Burnt, as an Imperfect Poem, by his last Will and Testament; was, because it did him a real Service as well as an Honour; that a Work should not be lost where his Divine Original was Celebrated in Verse, which had the Character of Immortality stamp'd upon it.

Neither were the great *Roman* Families which flourish'd in his time, less oblig'd by him than the Emperour. Your Lordship knows with what Address he makes mention of them, as Captains of Ships, or Leaders in the War; and even some of *Italian* Extraction are not forgotten. These are the single Stars which are sprinkled through the *Æneis*: But there are whole Constellations of them in the Fifth Book. And I could not but take notice, when I Translated it, of some Favourite Families to which he gives the Victory, and awards the Prizes, in the Person of his Heroe, at the Funeral Games which were Celebrated in Honour of *Anchises*. I insisit not on their Names: But am pleas'd to find the *Memmii* amongst them, deriv'd from *Mnestheus*, because *Lucretius* Dedicates to one of that Family, a Branch of which destroy'd *Corinth*. I likewise either found or form'd an Image to my self of the contrary kind; that those who lost the Prizes, were such as had disoblig'd the Poet, or were in disgrace with *Augustus*, or Enemies to *Mæcenas*: And this was the Poetical Revenge he took. For *genus irritabile Vatum*, as *Horace* says. When a Poet is throughly provok'd, he will do himself Justice, however dear it cost him, *Animamque, in Vulnere ponit.* I think these are not bare Imaginations of my own, though I find no trace of them in the Commentatours: But one Poet may judge of another by himself. The Vengeance we defer, is not forgotten. I hinted before, that the whole *Roman* People were oblig'd by *Virgil,* in deriving them from *Troy;* an Ancestry which they affected. We, and the *French* are of the same Humour: They would be thought to descend from a Son, I think, of *Hector:* And we wou'd have our *Britain,* both Nam'd and Planted by a descendant of *Æneas. Spencer* favours this Opinion what he can. His Prince *Arthur,* or whoever he intends by him, is a *Trojan.* Thus the Heroe of *Homer* was a *Grecian,* of *Virgil* a *Roman,* of *Tasso* an *Italian.*

—John Dryden, "Dedication of the Æneis," *The Works of Virgil in English* (1697), *The Works of John Dryden,* ed. William Frost (Berkeley: University of California Press, 1987), Vol. 5, pp. 281–83

❖

W. Y. SELLAR ON THE *AENEID* AS A NATIONAL EPIC

[W. Y. Sellar (1825–1890), a renowned classicist and lecturer, is the author of *The Roman Poets of the Republic* (1863) and *The Roman Poets of the Augustan Age: Horace and the Elegiac Poets* (1892). In this extract from his book on Vergil, Sellar, comparing the *Aeneid* to Homer, argues that it is an epic of national glory.]

The Iliad and the Odyssey are thus seen to be essentially epics of human life; the Aeneid is essentially the epic of national glory. The Iliad indeed is the noblest monument of the greatness, as it is of the genius, of the Greeks. And the Aeneid is much more than a monument of national glory. It is full of pathetic situations and stirring incidents which move our human compassion or kindle our sympathies with heroic action. But if we ask what are the most powerful sources of interest in the Greek and in the Roman epic respectively, the answer will be that in the first these spring immediately out of human life; in the second they spring out of the national fortunes. And this distinction is generally recognisable in the art, literature, and history of the two nations. This predominance of national interest and the presence of a large element of living modern interest in the treatment of an ancient legend separate the Aeneid still further from the Alexandrine epic and its later Roman imitations. The compliance with the conditions of epic poetry, as established by Homer and confirmed by the great law-giver of Greek criticism, equally separates it from the rude attempts of Ennius and Naevius, and from the poems which treat of historical subjects of a limited and temporary significance, such as the Pharsalia of Lucan and the Henriade of Voltaire. Though Virgil may be the most imitative, he is at the same time one of the most original poets of antiquity. We saw that he had produced a new type of didactic poetry. By the meaning and unity which he has imparted to his Greek, Roman, and Italian materials through the vivifying and harmonising agency of permanent national sentiment and of the immediate feeling of the hour, he may be said to have created a new type of epic poetry—to have produced a work of genius representative of his country as well as a masterpiece of art.

    —W. Y. Sellar, *The Roman Poets of the Augustan Age: Virgil* (Oxford: Clarendon Press, 1877 [3rd ed. 1897]), p. 324

❖

RICHARD HEINZE ON CENTRAL THEMES IN VERGIL'S EPIC

[Richard Heinze (1867–1929), a prominent German classical scholar, wrote numerous studies of classical authors and produced editions of their works. In the following extract from his book on Vergil, Heinze examines the ancient conventions of tragedy and points out that Vergil relies on astonishment, pity, and fear to convey his message.]

The aim of poetry as opposed to other verbal arts is to delight, and 'to shake the reader up', as we say, although Greek aesthetics used a different metaphor: 'to put the reader beside himself': ἡδονή [pleasure], also ψυχαγωγιά [literally, leading the soul] and ἔκπληξισ [excitement] are the continually recurring key words of post-Aristotelian theory. In tragedy the main weight falls completely on ἔκπληξισ, and since the aestheticians—since Aristotle, and even before his time—did not discriminate between epic and tragedy, this also held good for the epic. In itself ἐκπλήττειν [to excite, produce an emotional response] did not perhaps have to be bound up with the idea of violent excitement; serene beauty can also move the spirit very deeply. But one does not generally think of the word as embracing this possibility: one takes it to mean what had been established ever since Euripides as the specific effect of tragedy: the 'emotional, unexpected and surprising', or, as Plutarch once paraphrased it, 'the upsetting and amazing', or, to let Virgil's friend Horace have a word, it is the art of one *qui pectus inaniter angit, inritat, mulcet, falsis terroribus implet* [who torments my heart with illusions, grates, soothes, and fills with feigned terrors] (*Epodes* 2.1.211–12): a definition in which only *mulcere* [soothing] allows any small space for the gentler effects which are necessary for variety and recuperation. That certain basic aspects of Virgil's technique are decisively geared towards this goal is very obvious. In the present study of his epic technique, almost everything which we have had to label 'a dramatic touch' serves ἔκπληξισ: the writer of epic is attempting to rival the dramatist in arousing excitement, and therefore studies the secrets of his art. This can be felt most clearly in the structuring of the action: the striving after energetic forward movement, the strong emphasis on decisive moments, the stage-like structure of the smaller units, the preference of *peripeteia* [reversal] to a calmer, regular course, the struggle after surprising effects, the harsh light focussed on particular details by means of contrasts and climaxes—these are all characteristic of Virgil, and they are all borrowed from the dramatist's box of tricks. I do not need to go further with this (and related aspects) again here; but there is a wilder field which does require special attention.

At the centre of his theory of the effect of tragedy, Aristotle placed πάθοσ, pity and fear, which the poet must arouse in the audience. πάθοσ then continued to be regarded as the core of ἔκπληξισ: as time went on, emotion came to dominate poetry more and more; it became one of the highest aims of Virgilian epic too. There are two ways of achieving this aim: either by narrating events which arouse pity, anger, fear etc. in the audience; or by presenting the characters to us in an emotional state: the more vividly and visually this is done, the more easily we will identify with the character and share the depicted emotion, and, although much less intensely, ὁμοιοπαθεῖν [feel with them]. In many cases, both things happen, when there is a description not only of the exciting event but also of its effect on the participants: Virgil preferred this second, surer way.

The most noble tragic emotion, pity, also ranks highest in Virgil. For example, in Book 1 he is not satisfied with merely emphasizing the piteous aspects of the fate of Aeneas and the Trojans: episodic material, such as the narrative about Dido, the images in the temple at Carthage and the dialogue between Venus and Amor, becomes an extra source of pity. In the Sack of Troy, emphasis is laid on the piteous aspects of Hector's dream-appearance, the rape of Cassandra and the death of Priam; with the *prodigium* at the grave of Polydorus, the meeting with Andromache, the adventure with the Cyclops, where it would have been easy to concentrate on different emotions, the poet still appeals primarily to our pity. The sight of any suffering, such as that of a tortured animal or an invalid in pain, can awaken similar feelings of suffering in the onlooker; these feelings are intensified if they are combined with anger at the perpetrator of the suffering. This association of the ἐλεεινόν [piteous] and the δεινόν [fearsome] was also emphasized by the aestheticians, and turned to advantage in rhetoric. Thus the δείνωσισ [fearsomeness] of Neoptolemus' coarse cruelty and arrogance is an additional factor which increases our pity for Priam and Andromache; Sinon's perfidy, Pygmalion's criminal tryanny are painted in the blackest of colours in order to make us feel the fate of their victims more bitterly; even Juno's implacable hatred belongs in this category. At the same time, it may sometimes be merely the common pity of a tender heart; the whole person feels involved when not only his pity but also his love and admiration are directed towards the sufferer; it is only then that he really reaches the point of identifying with him. What led Virgil in the first place to ennoble his suffering characters in this way was probably his impulse to sympathize fully with them himself; but it is obvious how close this brings him to the requirement for the character of the tragic hero which Aristotle abstracted from Attic tragedy. It is this above all which distinguishes Dido from the suffering heroines of the most recent examples of pathetic narrative, that she not only appeals to other humans as a human being, but also, as a great-hearted and powerful yet feminine and gentle princess, she has won the admiration of the audience before it is time to win their pity. And Virgil does exactly the same whenever possible, even with figures in episodes: when we see Priam fall, we are not only touched by the disgraceful end of an old man: we have seen him face the enemy Sinon with courage, have admired the old man's heroic spirit, and are finally reminded that this poor unfortunate, whose corpse is not even granted a resting-place, was once the powerful ruler of Asia. Andromache's loyalty to her first husband, Palinurus' faithful care of his master, Euryalus' noble ambition and Nisus' faithful love for his friend, Lausus' sacrifice for his father—those are all features which make the poet's own creations really worthy of his pity in their suffering: they are also, one may add, the features which have continued to make these scenes of pathos effective through all the centuries since. Closely related to what we have just said is Virgil's treatment of the guilt which leads men to destruction. Hellenistic poetry had wallowed more and more in presenting *crimes de passion,* thereby seeking out the unnatural rather than avoiding it, in the belief that this would add to the pathetic effect. Virgil does allow past crimes to be mentioned, but he himself does not present them; how far removed is something like Dido's ἁμαρτία [fault] from the horrors with which the collection of Parthenius abounds. In other cases it is a question of lesser failings: Camilla, Nisus and Euryalus become the victims of their imprudent desires; the immoderate boldness of Pallas can hardly count as a failing; and in the case of the stupidity of the Trojans who pull their own destruction into the city, there can be no talk of tragic guilt. Here mankind faces the unfathomable decision of Fate, which also makes the innocent suffer; the poet knows the final purposes served by the fall of Troy and the wanderings of Aeneas: *tantae molis erat Romanam condere gentem* [such was the cost in heavy toil of beginning the life of Rome]; and it is just this glimpse of the future which prevents our justified pity from sinking to the agony of one condemned to watch the unnecessary and purposeless suffering of his fellow men.

For centuries, the *Aeneid* has been the paradigm of dramatic style in poetic narrative. To the question whether Virgil should be regarded as the actual creator of this style, a definite answer can hardly be given. This much is certain, that among the surviving monuments of Hellenistic poetry there is not one single poem which could lay claim to having been Virgil's model in every respect, or even in every important respect. To be sure, we have been able to draw attention to many minor points of comparison in Hellenistic literature, both earlier and later; but when Virgil copies Apollonius in one respect, and in another copies the originals of the *Wedding of Peleus* or the *Ciris*, it only highlights how different his aims are; Apollonius is totally lacking in the essential element, the dramatic character of the narrative; the later, extremely mannered epyllion, almost perverse in its composition, is the diametrical opposite of the Virgilian epic, which aims at a unified, harmonious effect; their treatment of the action cannot be compared in any way, since the fragmentary, arbitrary nature of the epyllion prevents us from speaking of a real story-line. As for the earlier short narrative poems of Hellenistic times, Virgil clearly did learn from them, above all in the very polished form of presentation, in the ἦθος [character] of the narrative, and possibly also in the striving for a unified effect; but for the rest, once again, their aims are as different as can be: they strive after ingenious enlivenment of the detail and a noble restraint in line and colour; his aims are a simple greatness, strong emotions, tension, excitement—in short, the ἐκπληκτικόν [astonishing].

> —Richard Heinze, *Virgil's Epic Technique* (1903), tr. Hazel and David Harvey (Berkeley: University of California Press, 1993), pp. 370–72

❖

Henry W. Prescott on Vergil's Delineation of Character

[Henry W. Prescott is the author of several papers on classical literature and *The Development of Virgil's Art* (1927), from which the following extract is taken. Here, Prescott examines the traditions of character development in classical literature and then studies Vergil's depiction of young men and women.]

It is from the standpoint of ⟨. . .⟩ ancient theory, with its emphasis upon general characterization, that we may best understand Virgil's achievement in the delineation of persons in his poem. The sum and substance of what we shall now illustrate in some detail is that Virgil, in portraying his characters, emphasizes general traits of character rather than individual qualities; there lies his weakness from a modern standpoint; yet within this broad description of his art we must leave room for a certain amount of clear individualism, and notably in the cases of several of the warriors of the last six books.

To illustrate his emphasis on general traits we may briefly consider the young men, the old men, the women, of the *Aeneid*. Virgil's sympathetic interest in young men is notable; he loved them; and, like Augustus, saw in them the hope of Rome's continued greatness. Ascanius, Pallas, Nisus, Euryalus, Lausus—they are among the most attractive figures of an epic mainly devoted to the achievements of matured heroic warriors. These five young fellows are in the main alike: they are all ideal types of hopeful, ambitious youth, ready to expose themselves to dangers to which they are not equal. Within this general likeness there is slight individual differentiation. Ascanius has lost his mother at an early age; he has been exposed to hardships in the voyage over sea and land; he has acquired a maturity beyond his years, proficiency in the hunt and on the battlefield; we see him grow from boyhood to youth, and in his final appearance in the ninth book his shot at Numanus marks the beginning of matured power; the god Apollo comes down to admonish him: "Such dawn of glory great Apollo's will concedes . . . but, tender youth, refrain hereafter from this war." It is this tenderness of youth which Euryalus embodies; he is old enough to compete in the foot race of the fifth book and to participate in the bold enterprise of the sally through the Latin camp in the ninth, but in the fifth book, like a child, he bursts into tears at being threatened with loss of a prize which he has won by Nisus' unsportsmanlike maneuver, and his childish delight in a shining helmet and his general imprudence ruin the effect of the bold sally with Nisus through the Latin camp. Lausus and Pallas have the same terrible thirst for achievement, but they are steadier, less reckless, than Euryalus; Pallas' bravery is exhibited in determined and consistent heroism; Lausus', in filial sacrifice of his life for his father's sake; but the difference is due to situation rather than to any essential variation of character.

Prominent old men are Ilioneus, Nautes, Evander, and above all, Anchises; speech and action, in their cases, are calm, well-considered, dispassionate, in sharp contrast with the impetuosity of the youngsters. They are directors, admonishers, prone to give others the benefits of their ripe experience and easily led to talk about the good old times; they are endowed with a deeper insight than others into the divine will and the decrees of Fate; Nautes has received this power from the goddess, Minerva; Anchises interprets omens, plays the rôle of prophet on occasion. All these old men are lineal descendants of Homer's Nestor, with all his wisdom and eloquence. Slightly differentiated is the aged king of the Latins, Latinus; he is an ideal king, pious, discreet, generous, gentle, upright; he has one conspicuous defect: he lacks the stiff backbone of consistency and determination; up to old age he has ruled over a peaceful folk; suddenly, when his physical strength is weak, he is exposed to a complicated situation; his family and people oppose him and demand war; he is not equal to the emergency.

The women of the poem are strikingly like one another; their common and almost exclusive trait is excitability; with them every feeling issues quickly in frenzy and passion; passion destroys their balance; when one of them is so affected, the frenzy quickly spreads to others. This emotional excitement is often justified; our present interest is simply in the general attribution of the quality to the sex as its distinguishing trait.

Virgil's oft-quoted description of woman as mutable and shift-
ing is exemplified in most of the women of the *Aeneid.*

—Henry W. Prescott, *The Development of Virgil's Art* (Chicago:
University of Chicago Press, 1927), pp. 466–68

❖

EDWARD KENNARD RAND ON VERGIL'S USE OF ROMAN GODS AND GODDESSES

[Edward Kennard Rand (1871–1945) was a prominent
classicist whose many publications include *Ovid and
His Influence* (1928) and *The Building of Eternal Rome*
(1943). In this extract from his study of Vergil, Rand
examines Vergil's use of the polytheistic Roman religion in the *Aeneid.*]

We must not forget that the gods take part in the drama of the
Aeneid. A measure of Dido's guilt reverts to Venus—not all, for
Dido, it would seem, had been ready of her own accord. But
Virgil's gods are not merely human passions writ large, adding
nothing to the plot but epic mechanism and the contrast of
shifted scenes; they are larger human actors, more powerful,
but submissive, like men, to the Fates. Standing in rank midway
between, they descend to the human plane, help or retard, and
withdraw. Their action has interest in itself and their characters
have personality. Thus Venus in the First Book seems charm-
ingly unintelligent in encouraging her son to run so great a
peril; she thinks, apparently, of Dido merely as an enemy who
may destroy the shipwrecked Trojans if she is not enamored of
Aeneas in time. The goddess does not consider that the hero's
infatuation delays the Fates and his ultimate triumph. Juno has
more sober sense: she will entangle him in the very trap that
Venus has set. Pretending indignation at such artifice, she proposes to her fair rival that the passion which Venus has aroused
be further strengthened by wedlock.

> Now thou hast what thou soughtest with all thy heart. Dido is
> afire with love and has sucked passion to the marrow of her

bones. Let us, therefore, you and I, rule with equal auspices this race conjoined. Let her be slave to a Phrygian lord, and entrust her Tyrians as dowry to thine hand.

Venus, perceiving the trick, answers with a smile:

> Who so mad as to spurn an offer like this, or prefer instead to take up arms against thyself—if only good fortune may attend the plan that thou proposest? But I drift doubtful of the Fates—whether Jove will that there should be one city for the Tyrians and the voyagers from Troy, or approve the union of their tribes and bonds of federation. Thou art his spouse, thou hast the right to test his temper with entreaty. Lead on: and I will follow.

Juno, oblivious to the delicious irony and coquetry of Venus's assent, undertakes to arrange things by herself. She sets the stage for the fatal hunt and the storm, for the meeting in the cave, for the liturgy which she will improvise to sustain the act. She presents the plan explicitly to Venus. And Venus "opposed not her request, but nodded, and smiled at the invention of such a snare." Venus smiles first at the cleverness of Juno's plans—for it is a downright good trick—but also because she perceives that it will all come back on Juno in the end. In short, Venus is far more sagacious than the reader suspected at the start.

This incident shows well enough the purpose of divine machinery in Virgil's drama. Gods complicate the plot, appearing as superhuman actors. They help or hinder mortals without being mere personifications of their qualities. They hasten or retard the Fates, without being mere symbols of ultimate purpose. Their coming shifts the scene to the radiancy of Olympus and gives the relief of contrast. In the scene before us, and elsewhere in the *Aeneid,* as in Homer, they afford comic relief for the setting of tragedy. Comedy for the gods; tragedy is reserved for mortal men—*miseri mortales*—whom Virgil's gods can sometimes pity too. In a word, Virgil's world has place for both the human and the divine.

—Edward Kennard Rand, *The Magical Art of Virgil* (Cambridge, MA: Harvard University Press, 1931), pp. 364–66

❖

T. S. Eliot on Vergil and Christianity

[T. S. Eliot (1888–1965), American-born modernist poet and playwright who spend most of his adult life in England, was also an important critic. He founded the quarterly magazine, the *Criterion,* and wrote *The Sacred Wood: Essays on Poetry and Criticism* (1920), *The Use of Poetry and the Use of Criticism* (1933), and other critical works. In this extract, Eliot examines the notion of *pietas* (the reverence due to the gods) and argues for a proto-Christian outlook in Vergil.]

The *pietas* is ⟨. . .⟩ explicable only in terms of *fatum.* This is a word which constantly recurs in the *Aeneid;* a word charged with meaning, and perhaps with more meaning than Virgil himself knew. Our nearest word is 'destiny', and that is a word which means more than we can find any definitions for. It is a word which can have no meaning in a mechanical universe: if that which is wound up must run down, what destiny is there in that? Destiny is not necessitarianism, and it is not caprice: it is something essentially meaningful. Each man has his destiny, though some men are undoubtedly 'men of destiny' in a sense in which most men are not; and Aeneas is egregiously a man of destiny, since upon him the future of the Western World depends. But this is an election which cannot be explained, a burden and responsibility rather than a reason for self-glorification. It merely happens to one man and not to others, to have the gifts necessary in some profound crisis, but he can take no credit to himself for the gifts and the responsibility assigned to him. Some men have had a deep conviction of their destiny, and in that conviction have prospered; but when they cease to act as an instrument, and think of themselves as the active source of what they do, their pride is punished by disaster. Aeneas is a man guided by the deepest conviction of destiny, but he is a humble man who knows that this destiny is something not to be desired and not to be avoided. Of what power is he the servant? Not of the gods, who are themselves merely instruments, and sometimes rebellious ones. The concept of destiny leaves us with a mystery, but it is a mystery not contrary to reason, for it implies that the world, and the course of human history, have meaning.

Nor does destiny relieve mankind of moral responsibility. Such, at least, is my reading of the episode of Dido. The love affair of Aeneas and Dido is arranged by Venus: neither of the lovers was free to abstain. Now Venus herself is not acting on a whim, or out of mischief. She is certainly proud of the destiny of her son, but her behaviour is not that of a doting mother: she is herself an instrument for the realization of her son's destiny. Aeneas and Dido had to be united, and had to be separated. Aeneas did not demur; he was obedient to his fate. But he was certainly very unhappy about it, and I think that he felt that he was behaving shamefully. For why else should Virgil have contrived his meeting with the Shade of Dido in Hades, and the snub that he receives? When he sees Dido he tries to excuse himself for his betrayal. *Sed me iussa deum*—but I was under orders from the gods; it was a very unpleasant decision to have imposed upon me, and I am sorry that you took it so hard. She avoids his gaze and turns away, with a face as immobile as if it had been carved from flint or Marpesian rock. I have no doubt that Virgil, when he wrote these lines, was assuming the role of Aeneas and feeling very decidedly a worm. No, destiny like that of Aeneas does not make the man's life any easier: it is a very heavy cross to bear. And I do not think of any hero of antiquity who found himself in quite this inevitable and deplorable position. I think that the poet who could best have emulated Virgil's treatment of this situation was Racine: certainly the Christian poet who gave the furious Roxane the blasting line '*Rentre dans le Néant d'où je t'ai fait sortir*' could, if anyone, have found words for Dido on this occasion.

What then does this destiny, which no Homeric hero shares with Aeneas, mean? For Virgil's conscious mind, and for his contemporary readers, it means the *imperium romanum*. This in itself, as Virgil saw it, was a worthy justification of history. I think that he had few illusions and that he saw clearly both sides of every question—the case for the loser as well as the case for the winner. Nevertheless even those who have as little Latin as I must remember and thrill at the lines:

> His ego nec metas rerum, nec tempora pono:
> Imperium sine fine dedi . . .
> Tu regere imperio populos, Romane, memento

[hae tibi erunt artes] pacique imponere morem,
parcere subiectis et debellare superbos . . .

I say that it was all the end of history that Virgil could be asked to find, and that it was a worthy end. And do you really think that Virgil was mistaken? You must remember that the Roman Empire was transformed into the Holy Roman Empire. What Virgil proposed to his contemporaries was the highest ideal even for an unholy Roman Empire, for any merely temporal empire. We are all, so far as we inherit the civilization of Europe, still citizens of the Roman Empire, and time has not yet proved Virgil wrong when he wrote *nec tempora pono: imperium sine fine dedi.* But, of course, the Roman Empire which Virgil imagined and for which Aeneas worked out his destiny was not exactly the same as the Roman Empire of the legionaries, the pro-consuls and governors, the business men and speculators, the demagogues and generals. It was something greater, but something which exists because Virgil imagined it. It remains an ideal, but one which Virgil passed on to Christianity to develop and to cherish.

>—T. S. Eliot, "Virgil and the Christian World" (1951), *On Poetry and Poets* (New York: Farrar, Straus & Cudahy, 1957), pp. 144–46

❖

GEORGE E. DUCKWORTH ON THE TRIPARTITE STRUCTURE OF THE *AENEID*

[George E. Duckworth (1903–1972) lectured at the American Academy at Rome, Harvard University, and Princeton University. He is the author of *The Nature of Roman Comedy* (1952), *Vergil and Classical Hexameter Poetry* (1969), and *Structural Patterns and Proportions in Vergil's* Aeneid (1962), from which the following extract is taken. Here, Duckworth traces a three-part structure in the *Aeneid,* with the deaths of Dido and Turnus framing the central portion that deals with the founding of Rome.]

Much has been written about Vergil's use of tragic drama, and Rand has aptly said: "Tragedy is an essential part of Vergil's poem—he was forever joining together what critics would keep asunder." The tripartite division of the *Aeneid* enables us to see more clearly the manner in which Vergil has framed his central message by the two tragedies of Dido and Turnus; both are protrayed most sympathetically and both meet death, not merely because they stand in the way of Aeneas and his mission and are, therefore, the victims of Divine Will, but also because each does the wrong thing and pays the penalty for his action. The two tragedies are not lacking in historical significance, however; just as Dido's death symbolizes the overthrow of Carthage by Rome (cf. the simile of the burning city in IV, 669ff.), so the defeat of Turnus suggests the later union of Romans and Latins and Roman supremacy in Italy.

The threefold division of the *Aeneid* also throws new light upon Vergil's use of epic material, especially that drawn from Homer. In the first and third sections of the poem many Homeric episodes, descriptions, and similes are incorporated into the action, but they are in general short passages (e.g., the story of Polyphemus in III and the breaking of the truce in XII). The epic material in these sections is adapted to the tragic nature of the context and is used primarily for the delineation of character, e.g., Aeneas' rage after the slaying of Pallas in X, not unlike that of Turnus and Aeneas; Turnus (324f.) avoids his opponent and rejoices in the opportunity to kill other warriors, but Aeneas (464ff.) considers himself bound by the terms of the truce and seeks Turnus alone.

In the central section (V–VIII) Vergil makes a very different use of Homeric material; in each of the books he adapts a lengthy passage:

V.	Funeral games (from *Iliad* XXIII)
VI.	Underworld scene (from *Odyssey* XI)
VII.	Catalogue (from *Iliad* II)
VIII.	Shield (from *Iliad* XVIII)

Here the long episodes are reworked and transformed for the glorification of Rome and its history, the portrayal of ancient Italy, and the greatness of the new era under Augustus who has triumphed over his enemies and introduced a new Golden Age of peace. The funeral games in Sicily in V are no exception but contain much of interest for the Romans of Vergil's day. This adaptation of long Homeric episodes for historical, patriotic, and nationalistic purposes is something unique and appears only in the central section of the poem. One other long episode, the night expedition in IX, is based upon Homer (the *Doloneia* in *Iliad* X), but this may be considered the exception to prove the rule: the story of Nisus and Euryalus, appearing in the opening book of the third part of the poem (the tragedy of Turnus), is itself a miniature tragedy, in which two characters meet disaster and death as the result of their own actions; this sets the tone for the final section of the *Aeneid,* when Turnus at the end of XII likewise pays the penalty for his own wrong act—the insolent treatment of the body of Pallas.

We are therefore entitled to look upon the *Aeneid* as a trilogy, with each third of the poem divided into four parts, or acts. The two tragedies of Dido and Turnus provide the framework for the central four books, which stress the patriotic and nationalistic themes, and at the very center of this section we find the speech of Anchises with its emphasis on Roman heroes, the achievement of Augustus, and the task of the Roman (VI, 760–853). *Aeneid* VI, called "the keystone of the whole poem," has been considered important in the twofold division of the epic; when we view the poem as a trilogy, we see that Vergil has stressed the importance of VI and especially Anchises' speech by its central position in the second section. In like manner, Eugene O'Neill in his trilogy *Mourning Becomes Electra* emphasized the sea background of the Mannon family and the symbolic motive of the sea as a means of escape and release by placing "the one ship scene at the center of the second play."

The alternating rhythm of the *Aeneid* and the more serious nature of the even-numbered books take on added significance when we look at the poem as a trilogy. Conway pointed out that each of the books with even numbers has a culminating point—II and IV in calamity, VI and VIII in revelation, X and XII in triumph. This grouping of the serious books has little importance in a twofold arrangement but becomes more meaningful in a tripartite division; the important books in each section of the trilogy are linked together by parallels and contrasts, just as are the corresponding books of each half in the twofold scheme.

—George E. Duckworth, *Structural Patterns and Proportions in Vergil's* Aeneid: *A Study in Mathematical Composition* (Ann Arbor: University of Michigan Press, 1962), pp. 11–12

❖

VIKTOR POSCHL ON VERGIL'S USE OF CHARACTERS IN THE *AENEID*

[Viktor Poschl, a prominent German classicist, is the author of numerous books on classical authors. In the following extract from his book on the *Aeneid,* Poschl argues that Vergil introduces significant individual traits when first introducing a character in his epic.]

Aeneas' first speeches reveal his basic character; they are inwardly and outwardly integral to the whole work because the poet concentrates completely on the essential and significant from the very beginning. However, this tendency to reveal basic traits of character and destiny upon the first appearance of an individual is also occasionally noticeable in Homer's much more loosely composed epic. It is seen, for example, in the sixth book of the *Iliad,* when Hector, failing to find Andromache at home, hears that she is neither with her family nor in the temple of Athena; on learning that the Trojans are being defeated and that the Achaeans' power is growing stronger, she has gone to the great tower of Illium. In her gesture of madly rushing to the wall, with the nurse carrying the child, her gentle and passionate soul is given expression. The poet need say nothing of her love, for the gesture expresses it better than words could. This is our introduction to Andromache! The scene simultaneously intimates Hector's destiny, for on a deeper level of understanding, Andromache's concern is revealed as tragic premonition.

The connection is not so obvious with the other characters in the *Iliad,* though their first appearance is characteristic. The manner in which Agamemnon screams at Chryses points up his violent and selfish nature, and Thetis instantly shows herself as a loving mother when in response to Achilles' prayer she rises like mist from the sea to caress her son. In his censure of Paris, Hector proves himself an unyielding defender of his people's honor and their true leader. In this expression of long-suppressed resentment he uncovers his passionate nature. But the connection with the development of the story is not so definite. The strict integration of detail with the whole, of words and gestures with character, of character with destiny, of destiny with the structure of the plot—all essentials in the *Aeneid*—are less well developed in the *Iliad.* So there is less immediacy in the establishment of the principle of classical composition, according to which each part receives its true importance only through its relation to the whole. The introduction of a course of events is more leisurely, so there is more opportunity for involvement with each character.

> —Viktor Poschl, *The Art of Vergil: Image and Symbol in the* Aeneid (1962), tr. Gerda Seligson (Ann Arbor: University of Michigan Press, 1966), pp. 42–43

❖

BROOKS OTIS ON HOMER AND VERGIL

[Brooks Otis, a noted classical scholar, is the author of *Ovid as an Epic Poet* (1966) and *Cosmos and Tragedy: An Essay on the Meaning of Aeschylus* (1981). In this extract from his book on Vergil, Otis investigates the influence of Homer on Vergil, showing how Vergil adapted mythic structure to political and psychological ends.]

Virgil had given a quite new meaning, a thoroughly contemporary meaning, to the didactic form.

This is the light then in which we must look at the *Aeneid* if we are really to understand it. Virgil used Homer here, much as he had used Hesiod, Nicander or Aratus in the *Georgics*. In other words Homer gave him a form, something of a style, a great deal of content, but not the essential idea or meaning, not the ideological *truth* he wanted to convey. He saw (I would suspect very early in the game, though we can never be certain) that he could not directly *Homerize* modern or historical material or, in other words, write of Augustus as if he were really the associate of Hector, Achilles and the gods on Olympus. Hence his question was: how can I use the Homeric counters as effective *symbols* of Augustan realities? Or even more specifically: how can I put the basic Augustan schema of the *Georgics* into such symbols? The great difference of course was that Homer had written of human beings, not of soils, cattle, and bees. It was the difference, in other words, between human and nonhuman symbols. Or, even more exactly, it was the difference between symbols and more or less *exemplary* men and women. It was in this way, as I conceive it, that Virgil looked at the problem, though we cannot of course draw too many conclusions as to how far he consciously articulated it to himself.

At any rate the *Aeneid* makes sense when seen in this perspective. Aeneas is, in effect, an Augustan type—a *divine man,* not necessarily copied after the Emperor himself but embodying the Augustan ruler-ideal—who emerges out of Homeric society and, in virtue of his emergence, imposes upon a more primitive but still quasi-Homeric society a defeat that is the means to unity, peace and civilization on the Augustan plan. But he does this only because he *becomes* Augustan, that is, because he is 'reborn' at the crisis of his career by the acquisition of an historical perspective which includes Augustus and the Augustan *pax Romana*. Only so can he bring the civilized future to bear upon the primitive or Homeric present in which he, as *dramatis persona,* is supposed to stand. In this sense we can partially describe the *Aeneid* as the creation of Roman civilization out of Homeric barbarism. It is not, however, so much the contrast of the Homeric and Augustan eras in themselves that Virgil is interested in, as the contrast of human ideals and motivations: he is, in short, concerned with Aeneas as the opposite and opponent of such men and women as Dido and Turnus and, perhaps above all, as the man who overcomes the Dido and Turnus inside himself.

It was not, in theory at least, too difficult to devise a *plot* that would carry Virgil's ideological, Augustan meaning. The Homeric motifs had to be recast and united to Roman legend, the Augustan present had to be introduced by prophecy and prophetic scenes, the role of the *Nekuia* had to be wholly transformed, &c. But all of this was more a matter for ingenuity than poetical genius. The real problem was to make the plot function in a poem. This meant the achievement of credibility by creating the right poetical atmosphere or, more exactly, the directing point of view that would give poetical unity to such an intricate and necessarily artificial mixture of ideas and motifs. Here was where Virgil's subjective style and psychologically continuous narrative became of paramount importance. Had he envisaged his plot in the objective manner of Homer and Apollonius and told it as a simple narrative of real people and real events, he would surely have accomplished only a grotesque failure. Actually, as a Roman, Virgil inherited a kind of subjective style (in the sense that I have set forth in chap. iii), but he certainly added a quite new dimension to what he got from Lucretius or Catullus or others. So far as we can tell, he alone employed the kind of sustained empathy that permitted a psychologically continuous narrative. But it was above all his combination of empathy with editorial 'sympathy' that gave him control over his Homeric material, enabled him to *correlate* mythological symbols with psychological events and made possible his marvellous transformation of epic conventions. It is on his 'subjective style' in short that his whole intricate structure of symbols and motifs depends. Without this, his plot *per se* would be a curiously artificial thing, a flimsy paste-and-scissors job that could not create or sustain any sort of poetical illusion.

But we must not therefore assume that the whole *Aeneid* is an operatic *trompe l'oeil,* an artificial combining of Homeric and Augustan elements by various stylistic tricks. The Virgilan empathy and sympathy are quite real: he really does see into and feel with the hearts of his characters. He really does see his world in deeply emotional terms, really does transform Homeric motifs and similes into evocative symbols of his own feelings and thoughts. Truth can be subjectively as well as objectively conveyed. Virgil is not false because he is not Homer.

—Brooks Otis, *Virgil: A Study in Civilized Poetry* (Oxford: Clarendon Press, 1963), pp. 384–86

❖

CHARLES PAUL SEGAL ON HISTORY AND TRAGEDY IN THE *AENEID*

[Charles Paul Segal (b. 1936), a longtime professor of classics at Brown University, is now a professor of classics and comparative literature at Princeton University. He is the author of many studies, including *Poetry and Myth in Ancient Pastoral* (1981), *Orpheus: The Myth of the Poet* (1989), and *Singers, Heroes, and Gods in the* Odyssey (1994). In this extract, Segal points out that, along with his sense of the grandeur of Roman history, Vergil exhibits a tragic awareness of human misery.]

"There is a peculiarly comforting feeling experienced by a whole nation," wrote Goethe in *Dichtung und Wahrheit,* "when somebody succeeds in calling up its history in a telling and sympathetic manner. It rejoices in the ancestral virtues, and smiles at the ancestral failings, as at things of the past. A work of this kind is bound to reap sympathetic applause, and so I was able to rejoice in a considerable success." Had Vergil lived as long as Goethe he might have explained the success of the *Aeneid* in terms similar to these reflections of his on the popularity of his early *Götz.* In Vergil's case, however, all we have is the vague and disturbing account of his deathbed wish to burn the manuscript. Though we have no way of knowing whether Vergil's misgivings lay with the style or the matter, or both, we have come to doubt some of the traditional reasons for the popularity and greatness of the *Aeneid.*

Generations of schoolboys have been piously taught to read Vergil as the great celebrator of the glory of Rome, the confident exponent of Rome's proud advance from tribe to nation. Such interpretations may have fired the blood of nineteenth- and early twentieth-century Americans and Englishmen stirred by the creation of the national empires going on before their eyes. But a generation which daily sees the continued existence of mankind threatened by the fact of nations and empire may have a sense of elements in the *Aeneid* less clearly visible to readers of half a century ago.

It would, of course, be a patent falsehood to deny the fervor of Vergil's hope in the Augustan empire. To one whose boyhood and early manhood had been ravaged by the seemingly endless violence of the civil wars, the promise of peace and order was among the intensest of wishes:

> di patrii, Indigetes, et Romule Vestaque mater,
> quae Tuscum Tiberim et Romana Palatia servas,
> hunc saltem everso iuvenem succurrere saeclo
> ne prohibete. satis iam pridem sanguine nostro
> Laomedonteae luimus periuria Troiae.   (*Georg.* 1.498–502)

> (Gods of our country, native gods [?], and Romulus and mother Vesta who keeps the Tuscan Tiber and the Roman Palatine, prevent not this youth at least from coming to aid our overturned age. Enough have we long ago paid with our blood for the perjuries of Laomedon's Troy.)

But along with the abiding value of the promise of order, there is another side to the *Aeneid* of which interpreters in recent years have become increasingly aware: a pessimism about the cost of history, an acute sensitivity to the suffering of the individuals who participate in it. One need point only to the bitter and haunting last line, *vitaque cum gemitu fugit indignata sub umbras* (12.952: "And with a groan his life fled outraged to the shades below").

This negative element—the source of Vergil's tragic sense—pervades the poem, more strongly than most earlier interpreters have admitted. And since the human value of the past exists largely in relation to the present which restores it to life, we are not "distorting" Vergil in exploring that aspect of his work any more than the nineteenth century did in stressing his confidence in the progress toward empire. It is rather that we have become responsive to a different and, it is hoped, wider range of Vergil's art. To neglect this aspect of the poem only results in a false and simplistic reading or, by reaction, a premature rejection of Vergil altogether, such as Graves' recent one-sided attack on Vergil, the "antipoet" (*Oxford Address on Poetry,* 1962). Graves' "antipoet," however, is not Vergil as we have him, he is perhaps the Vergil that was expounded to Graves in school, a *Vergilius dimidiatus.*

The problem of Vergil's sense of the tragedy of history rests heavily upon the Sixth Book. In structure and meaning it is the center of the poem; and, in its famous pageant of Roman history and its prophecy of the Golden Age to be brought by Augustus, it deals more explicitly than any other part of the poem with the thinly balanced ledger of history. But the Sixth Book also contains one of the most poignant statements in the poem about the value of the effort (719–21). In this tension between the epic celebration of the glory of the Roman achievement and the question of the suffering it entails lie both the difficulty and the greatness of the *Aeneid.*

> —Charles Paul Segal, "*Aeternum per Saecula Nomen,* the Golden Bough and the Tragedy of History: Part I," *Arion* 4, No. 4 (Winter 1965): 617–18

❖

G. KARL GALINSKY ON THE *PIETAS* OF AENEAS

[G. Karl Galinsky (b. 1942) is chairman of the department of classics at the University of Texas at Austin. He is the author of *The Herakles Themes: Adaptations of the Hero in Literature from Homer to the Twentieth Century* (1972) and *Ovid's* Metamorphoses: *An Introduction to the Basic Aspects* (1975). In this extract from his book on Vergil, Galinsky examines the importance of *pietas* in the *Aeneid* and in Roman culture as a whole.]

Some of the most perceptive remarks on Vergil's intent are still those by Tiberius Claudius Donatus:

> For his task was to present Aeneas in such a way that he might prove to be a worthy parent and ancestor of Augustus in whose honor the epic was written. Because Vergil was to convey to posterity that this very man, Aeneas, had emerged as the founder of the *imperium Romanum,* he doubtless had to present him, as he did, as being free from all blame and as the worthy object of great praise . . .
>
> By his magical art Vergil clears Aeneas of these accusations (of treason). This he does not only with a programmatic declaration in the very first lines of the epic, but his justification is interspersed throughout all books. Finally—and this is the hallmark of a man greatly skilled in rhetoric—he openly states the things that could not be denied, eliminates the accusation, and then turns it into praise, in order to make Aeneas in numerous ways outstanding for the very reasons which could give rise to his detraction.

Ut dignus Caesari, in cuius honorem haec scribebantur, parens et auctor generis praeberetur—this explains, more than anything else, why Aeneas was portrayed as *pius* in the epic, and why *pius* Aeneas became so important a theme in the artistic and numismatic imperial propaganda. Nor is it coincidental that the iconography of Pietas did not take on definite form until the Principate. As Aeneas throughout the epic is in many ways identified with Augustus, so Aeneas' *pietas* typifies that of the ruling monarch. Augustus proudly relates in the *Monumentum Ancyranuum* (34) that a golden shield had been set up in his honor in the Curia Iulia because of his *virtus, clementia, iustitia,* and *pietas.* The presentation of this shield was made in 27 B.C.—the very year in which Vergil began composing the epic whose hero was the Julian ancestor. The eagerness of Augustus, *templorum omnium conditor aut restitutor* (Livy 4.20.7), to be considered as *pius* is reflected even in Tacitus' terse account of the emperor's reign. The mention of Augustus' *pietas* is the very first point made in the enumeration of the emperor's praiseworthy deeds (*Annals* 1.9) as well as in their rebuttal: some charged that Augustus assumed his *pietas erga patrem* merely as a mask (*Annals* 1.10). Tacitus here "records faithfully the diverse attitudes to Augustus that were current at the time of his death."

Of course this is not to affirm the romantic prejudice that Vergil was merely an imperial propagandist. Rather, the salient fact with which we are here concerned is that his choice of Aeneas as the official ancestor of Rome was not, in the first century B.C., the matter of course it has been regarded in retrospect. Meanwhile, it suffices to say that by the end of the first century B.C., Trojan descent had been the jealously guarded prerogative of a few noble families, the *familiae Troianae,* for the better part of two centuries. Therefore there was at least the possibility that another hero, like Hercules, Odysseus, or Evander, might have been accepted as the popular ancestor of all the Roman people. But since it was Octavian, a member of the Julian family, who asked Vergil to write the epic, Aeneas was selected because of his assumed connection with the *gens* Julia, and "once the choice was made, all the power of Augustan propaganda was used to publicize it and make the Aeneas legend popular." This effort in no way detracts from Vergil's achievement; the popularity, for instance, of the *Odissia Latina* made it a necessity and without it the *Aeneid* might have become no more than the family bible of the Julian *gens.*

We can see now, however, why Aeneas was meant to prefigure Augustus. *Pietas* was the final of the virtues mentioned on Augustus' Golden Shield, and perhaps the most important and inclusive. It reminded the Romans—as did the *pius* Aeneas—that the emperor, *divi filius,* was at once the object of *pietas* from his subjects, and an example to them of *pietas* toward the gods. For this reason the emperors continued to place programmatic emphasis on the *pietas* theme; among the most conspicuous examples are the Ara Pietatis, built by Claudius, Commodus' title *Pietatis Auctor,* and the coins with Aeneas and Anchises, and with Livia as *Pietas.*
    —G. Karl Galinsky, *Aeneas, Sicily and Rome* (Princeton: Princeton University Press, 1969), pp. 50–53

❖

[W. R. Johnson (b. 1933), a professor of classical languages and literature at the University of Chicago, is
the author of *Luxuriance and Economy: Cicero and the
Alien Style* (1971), *The Idea of Lyric: Lyric Modes in
Ancient and Modern Poetry* (1982), and *Momentary
Monsters: Lucan and His Heroes* (1987). In this extract
from his book on the *Aeneid*, Johnson maintains that
Vergil was both a product of the Augustan age and
shaped the age itself.]

Great writers are never the products of the times they live in,
though they often seem so because they reflect—indirectly but
brilliantly—the events, the common attitudes, hopes, and fears
of their contemporaries. But they do not merely react to events
or passions or "doctrines of the times" as purely popular writers do; they also react against events and contemporary attitudes and use these critical reactions to shape something
permanent and true out of the ephemeral. All these true tru-
isms mean here is that the term "the Augustan Age" identifies
a propaganda device that was very successful and is now a
handy but somewhat deceptive category for people who are
engaged in writing or lecturing about the poetry or the art or
the political events or social patterns that existed within a certain span of time. The only world that Vergil lived in was the
poetic one he created out of the various dying and evolving
worlds that he inhabited with his contemporaries. In this chap-
ter I shall examine some of the raw materials that these partial
worlds offered Vergil when he began to fashion, and as he kept
fashioning, his epic; in looking at these raw materials I have
two aims.

First, I think it is important to qualify the idea that Vergil is an
Augustan poet. Whatever its connections with the Ara Pacis,
which it partly inspired, it would be more nearly correct to say
that the *Aeneid* created the Augustan Age than to say that the
Augustan Age produced, in any way, the *Aeneid*. It was the
passionate concern and the imagination of Vergil that supplied
an intellectual coherence to a period of time that would other-
wise have lacked it, and of the few contemporaries of Vergil

who cared about that coherence, Augustus took from it only what interested him. It was the mind and heart of Vergil that brought intellectual and aesthetic order to the confused and anxious times in which he lived.

Second, since in many of the configurations it presents, Vergil's epic is about degenerations and renewals; since in at least one of its aspects it ponders the tragic failure of classical humanism to confront its own weaknesses and the new dangers that threaten it from without, it seems useful for a reading of the poem to emphasize that Vergil lived in an age when the shared metaphors that any society requires in order to exist were disintegrating and when, therefore, Vergil and his contemporaries were beginning to inhabit separate and divided worlds. This problem did not worry Lucretius, who had no use for this kind of metaphor or for the kind of society that required metaphors for its existence. But the tough independence of Lucretius, rare in any age, was clearly very rare in the late republic and early empire, and Vergil was worried about the disintegration of the shared metaphors and their community. The *Aeneid* records, among other things, Vergil's effort to close with and to master this worry over the divisions of a unity he believed in. And the dying and divided worlds that Vergil lived in were only renewed and unified by Vergil's hard-won ability to admit the fact of their death and division. When we talk of the Augustan Age, whether we know it or not, it is often this single act of self-discipline and courage that we have in mind.

—W. R. Johnson, *Darkness Visible: A Study of Vergil's* Aeneid (Berkeley: University of California Press, 1976), pp. 135–36

❖

GORDON WILLIAMS ON IRONY IN THE *AENEID*

[Gordon Williams, a professor of classics at Yale University, is the author of several volumes on Latin literature, including *The Nature of Roman Poetry* (1970), *Change and Decline: Roman Literature in the Early Empire* (1978), and *Figures of Thought in Roman Poetry*

(1980). In this extract from his book on the *Aeneid,*
Williams points to the several instances of irony in the
Aeneid, noting that they compel a rereading of the text
to reveal hidden meanings.]

A frequent feature of poetry from Catullus to the death of
Horace is that its composition requires a reader to suspend
judgment on the interpretation of a particular passage or idea
until more, or often all, of the poem has been read. The effect
is to sustain the energy of a poem by arousing an expectation
that is not satisfied in the immediate context. When this figure
is transferred to epic, the change in scale dictates a considerable variation in technique. Sometimes it may even happen
that the question or doubt is not aroused in the reader's mind
until he reaches the point where, had the expectation been in
his mind, it would have been satisfied. Such instances compel a
re-reading, and a number of examples of the technique have
already been noticed. Especially significant is Turnus' speech to
his sister Juturna in which he confesses that he has known her
identity all along and calls into question the accounts that have
been given of the deaths of two of his friends.

Of course, in poetry on the scale of epic, the effect can also
be seen, for instance, in certain cases of irony, for the irony
cannot be recognised until the situation that will reveal it as
such has been reached. Aeneas says, in his first speech to Dido
(1.607–10):

> "in freta dum fluvii current, dum montibus umbrae
> lustrabunt convexa, polus dum sidera pascet,
> semper honos nomenque tuum laudesque manebunt,
> quae me cumque vocant terrae."

> "As long as rivers shall flow into the ocean, as long as shadows
> shall move over mountain slopes, as long as clouds shall nour-
> ish the stars, for ever shall you be honoured, respected and
> revered whatever lands call me on."

The hyperbole may suggest a rash formulation, but those
words are only dramatically ironic in the light of Book 4 and
the particular way in which the tragedy of Dido takes place. For
Dido will feel dishonoured by Aeneas' treatment of her to such
an extent that she is compelled to suicide.

Another example can be seen in the words of Latinus as he praises his people and his kingdom (7.202–04):

> "ne fugite hospitium, neve ignorate Latinos
> Saturni gentem haud vinclo nec legibus aequam,
> sponte sua veterisque dei se more tenentem."

> "Shun not our hospitality and understand that the Latins are the race of Saturn, a race that is not righteous by any compulsion of law, but is self-controlled of its own free will and after the manner of the god of old."

It will turn out that the Latins indeed do exercise free will and are lawless, but not in the way that Latinus intended. They will break the sacred bond of hospitality and they will also break a solemn truce. Full appreciation of the dramatic irony in Latinus' words does not come until well into Book 12. There is something like authorial irony, too, in the case of Latinus. After the second prooemium to the *Aeneid* (7.37–45), we read (45–46):

> Rex arva Latinus et urbes
> iam senior longa placidas in pace regebat.

> King Latinus, now advanced in years, ruled over fields and cities that were quiet in a long-standing peace.

This seems to be a statement that is to be taken as authorially objective. But in fact it expresses the complacent viewpoint of Latinus, and the nature of the peace only becomes clear later. The Latins are at peace simply because Turnus is fighting their war with Etruria for them. Allecto disguised as Calybe says to him in a dream (7.425–26):

> "i nunc, ingratis offer te, inrise, periclis;
> Tyrrhenas, i, sterne acies, tege pace Latinos."

> "Go on then, place yourself in dangers that win you no gratitude—they only mock you; go on, lay low the battle-lines of Etruria, keep the Latins safely at peace."

Nor is that all. Tiber reveals later to Aeneas that Evander and his people (8.55) *hi bellum adsidue ducunt cum gente Latina* "have been waging continuous war with the Latin race." It is true that the war turns out to be insignificant, because Evander is old and his forces small; they are simply ignored by the complacent Latinus. His idealism is further undercut by Numanus' boastful words later (9.607–13):

> "at patiens operum parvoque adsueta iuventus
> aut rastris terram domat aut quatit oppida bello.
> omne aevum ferro teritur, versaque iuvencum
> terga fatigamus hasta, nec tarda senectus
> debilitat viris animi mutatque vigorem:
> canitiem galea premimus, semperque recentis
> comportare iuvat praedas et vivere rapto."

> "Our youth is inured to toil and accustomed to frugality, and either tames the ground with harrows or makes cities quake with their warfare. All our life is spent with weapons and we use a reversed spear to goad the backs of our oxen. Old age comes late and does not weaken the powers of our spirit or alter its vigour. We cover gray hair with the helmet and it is our delight to haul back ever more loot and to live on what we have stolen."

Numanus is, of course, contrasting his own people with the effeminate Trojans, but the further unspoken contrast with the complacent portrait given by Latinus is shockingly ironic. There is, however, a further powerful dramatic irony in Numanus' words, because it is exactly that desire for loot that will be the immediate cause of Turnus' death (no less than that of the ideal Italian Camilla).

In these passages a suspension of judgment or—what amounts to the same thing—a second reading reveals a hidden dimension in an earlier passage when it is brought into confrontation with a later one. There are several major cases in the *Aeneid,* however, where a reader has to exercise retrospective judgment on a question of real magnitude, in such a way as to be compelled to interpret an earlier stage of the text in the light of a later, or to read what was not said in an earlier stage back into that stage on evidence supplied by a later passage.

—Gordon Williams, *Technique and Ideas in the* Aeneid (New Haven: Yale University Press, 1983), pp. 40–42

❖

[Jasper Griffin, Professor of Classical Languages and Literature at Balliol College, Oxford, is the author of *Homer on Life and Death* (1980), *The Mirror of Myth* (1986), and *Latin Poets and Roman Life* (1985), from which this extract is taken. Here, Griffin compares Aeneas to Odysseus and Achilles and then examines some of the other characters in the *Aeneid*, especially Turnus.]

In the first half of the *Aeneid* the main model for the experiences of Aeneas is of course the Odysseus of the *Odyssey;* in the second half he bears a general resemblance to the Achilles of the *Iliad,* culminating in his slaying of Turnus in a scene evocative of the slaying of Hector. But the picture is far more complex. His relationship to Dido and Lavinia causes his enemies to see him as Paris, the foreigner who seduces or abducts local queens (4.215; cf. 9.592ff.). From another point of view he plays the role of Menelaus, demanding the wife who is kept from him in a foreign city. Indeed, the scene in Book 12 where he is wounded in a breach of the truce puts him in the role of the Menelaus of *Iliad* 4. With Dido, Aeneas is not only Odysseus (telling his adventures to the Phaeacians and having to disentangle himself from Calypso), but he also plays the role of Apollonius' Jason. Jason both abandons Hypsipyle (Book 1) and beds with Medea in a cave (Book 4), so that we have echoes of two relationships of Apollonius' hero, not one. When he comes to visit Evander, we see him take on some of the colouring of Telemachus visiting Nestor and Menelaus; when he celebrates games at Actium, as we have seen, he foreshadows Augustus, while as for Heracles, 'Virgil assimilates Aeneas to Heracles from the very beginning.' He is a Trojan patriot, an Italian (descended from the Italian Dardanus), a Roman, an Augustan.

The other important characters are no less complex. Turnus, who dies the death of Hector, was predicted by the Sibyl to become an Achilles, and was born of a goddess as Achilles was (6.89f.). The champion of Italy against the invader, he traces his descent back to Agamemnon's city of Mycenae (7.372). Dido at her first appearance is seen in the light of Nausicaa; then she entertains Aeneas just as Arete and Alcinous, queen and king of the Phaeacians, entertained Odysseus. She attempts to hold on to him, like Calypso; she is united with him in a cave, like Medea; when she is abandoned she echoes the abandoned Ariadne of Catullus 64 (4.316). But she also incarnates the national enemy in Carthage, she is a founder of a city like Aeneas himself, and when she comes to review her own career before her suicide she speaks in the style of the Roman general in his *elogium,* his epitaph for himself (4.655f.) Through the figure of the foreign queen who tries to seduce the Roman from his destiny and his home we feel a certain vibration of the unforgettable Cleopatra.

All this is perhaps obvious enough, but the important thing is what Virgil does with all this learning and all these parallels. As we saw, those who believe in typological explanations see this matter as essentially simple: according to Knauer, for example, Virgil shows how greater Rome exceeds and eclipses lesser Troy, and, according to Perret, Virgil presents in Aeneas a hero who assumes the qualities of earlier heroes such as Odysseus and Achilles, but who supersedes them. The reality is more complex and more interesting. When Dido appears in the light of the young Nausicaa or the touching Ariadne, part of our response to her derives from our response to those models and to the emotional resonance which they bring with them. When she turns to magic like Medea or Circe, we experience a different emotion: the pity appropriate to a young girl is overlaid by the horror and revulsion we feel for a witch. When she struggles to retain her dignity while at the same time asking him to stay, memories of our attitude towards Calypso in *Odyssey* 5 are aroused; when she curses the hero and Rome and invokes the idea of Hannibal as her avenger, we are meant to feel the chill of fear which that terrible memory always had for a Roman.

> —Jasper Griffin, "The Creation of Characters in the *Aeneid*," *Latin Poets and Roman Life* (London: Duckworth, 1985), pp. 193–95

❖

[Francis Cairns is a professor of classics at the University of Leeds in Leeds, England, and the author of *Generic Composition in Greek and Roman Poetry* (1972) and *Tibullus: A Hellenistic Poet at Rome* (1979). In this extract from his book on the *Aeneid,* Cairns studies Jupiter as depicted in the epic, showing that his role differs significantly from the way Zeus was portrayed in Homer.]

As has often been observed, the Jupiter of the *Aeneid* is, because of intervening hellenistic developments, close to being a monotheistic 'God' and far away from Homer's Zeus. The distribution of references to Jupiter's kingship is significant in this respect: they are missing from Books 5, 8, 9 and 11 and most concentrated in Book 10, with five examples. Thus, although some do simply have local significance only, the position of many relates to Jupiter's role as the cosmic promoter of reconciliation, peace and concord, a power united in will and purpose with fate. Of the two in Book 1, Juno's reminder to Aeolus that *divum pater atque hominum rex* has appointed him controller of the winds (65) is a persuasive *suggestio falsi* (for Jupiter would not approve of her request) and it is yet another implicit comment on Aeolus' failure to control his subjects. Balancing it is 229ff., where Venus reminds Jupiter of his cosmic rule and relationship with destiny. Book 2 contrasts two exercises of Jupiter's power of deciding the destiny of two individuals, Anchises (648f.) and Creusa (778f.). Both show Jupiter as directing the fate of significant characters at significant points. At 4.268f. this is seen again: when Jupiter sends Mercury to intervene directly and to command Aeneas to leave Carthage, the god reinforces his message by referring to Jupiter and to his role as ruler of the universe.

The Giants' attack on Jupiter's kingdom at 6.582–4 probably has more to do with contemporary political allegory than with the plot of the *Aeneid,* especially since Book 6 is more concerned with the royal status of Dis, the Jupiter of the Underworld. But Juno's dismissal of Allecto, after her work is done, with the comment that her further presence on earth would not please *summi regnator Olympi* (7.557–9) is an admission that their joint activities breach the order of things. Book 10, with its five examples, portrays Jupiter in his role as cosmic ruler and reconciler at its beginning (2). Although he later professes neutrality as between the Trojans and the Italians (*rex Iuppiter omnibus idem./fata viam invenient*, 112f.), the setting and atmosphere of the opening council of the gods and the consciousness of future history which attends it anticipate the final solution of the conflict in Book 12. This is why the kingship of Jupiter accompanies two interventions by him in Book 10 over important individuals (437, 621), in both of which contexts the role of the *fata* is directly or obliquely stressed (438, 624); and this is why Jupiter's kingship appears even in the mouth of the *contemptor deum* Mezentius (743). The last example in the *Aeneid* again involves intervention by Jupiter, this time to end Juturna's aid to Turnus (12.849). Interestingly Virgil abstains from exploiting kingship verbally during the ultimate divine reconciliation of Book 12. Instead, and to stress the genuineness of the reconciliation, he exploits the familial aspects of the renewed concord between his royal protagonists, Jupiter and Juno.

The kingship of other gods in the *Aeneid* is not unimportant; but its importance is limited. Whereas Jupiter's kingship is universal and monarchical in a true sense, that of the rest is local and subordinate. Such emphasis as is placed on other gods' kingship reflects in part the *Aeneid's* homeric background, and in part its overall desire to give prominence to kingship. A brief summary will suffice. Of the other gods, Juno is naturally referred to most frequently in this role after Jupiter; and her progression as a 'king' reverses that of her protégée, Dido. While Dido, as will be seen, deteriorates as a monarch, Juno improves as such, lays aside her *ira*, which is the principal divine obstacle to the fulfilment of the will of Jupiter and Fate, and so is ultimately reconciled with Jupiter and takes her place as Juno Regina in the highest ranks of the Roman pantheon. This formulation can stand despite the facts of future history, when Juno will be ranged against Rome in the Punic wars. Recent scholarship has rightly insisted that nevertheless the reconciliation in the *Aeneid* is in essence genuine. In contrast to Juno's progress, the *furor*, i.e. the excessive amorous passion of Dido, which like *ira* breaches the royal virtue of self-control (σωφροσύνη), brings Dido to destruction.

—Francis Cairns, *Virgil's Augustan Epic* (Cambridge: Cambridge University Press, 1989), pp. 25–27

❖

R. O. A. M. LYNE ON VERGIL'S USE OF LANGUAGE

[R. O. A. M. Lyne teaches at Balliol College, Oxford. He has written *The Latin Love Poets: From Catullus to Horace* (1980), *Further Voices in Vergil's* Aeneid (1986), and *Horace: Behind the Public Library* (1995). In this extract from his book on the *Aeneid,* Lyne compares Vergil's use of language to Horace's, contending that they both rely on the skillful use of ordinary speech.]

Horace makes poetry out of 'ordinary words' to a remarkable degree, and is perhaps most striking for his use of prosaisms. Investigators of Vergil's vocabulary have likewise established that in spite of being 'amantissimus uetustatis' 〈"a great lover of antiquity"〉 (Quintilian 1.7.18) Vergil relies remarkably little, considering his genre, on archaism and other poetic diction; like Horace he favours the use of 'iunctura', 'combination', to produce poetry from 'ordinary words'; and like Horace he is receptive to prosaic diction in particular and to the effects that can be gained with it. Some characteristic Vergilian techniques of combination, operating for the most part with 'ordinary words', are illustrated in this book.

It seems to me that Vergil's procedures with language are often more extreme than Horace's. Vergil uses combinations not only as Horace to 'make a familiar word new', to freshen it, but to extort novelty of sense, to wrest from a word some quite unexpected meaning. Horace can put prosaic (or colloquial) words to work in spite of their unpromising familiarity; Vergil can more vigorously exploit them. Because of the more

extreme nature of such techniques, I adopt assertive, even violent metaphors to describe them: 'extortion', 'exploitation'.

But not all Vergil's methods merit such descriptions. His use
of the traditional simile is characterized rather by discretion and
guile. Discreetly and guilefully 'narrative through imagery'
accompanies more forceful methods of making poetry, on key
occasions linking up with them. Guilefully, too, Vergil may use
(say) one of his exploitations as an incitement to us to pursue a
sequence of related effects; and he may discreetly persuade a
neutral word to acquire some special sense over a stretch of
text.

The total result is dense, teasing, often puzzling. Vergil can
seem, and has seemed even in antiquity, elusive or obscure.
—R. O. A. M. Lyne, *Words and the Poet: Characteristic
Techniques of Style in Vergil's* Aeneid (Oxford: Clarendon Press,
1989), pp. 17–18

❖

Susan Ford Wiltshire on Vergil's Attitude toward Women

[Susan Ford Wiltshire (b. 1941) is a professor of classics
at Vanderbilt University and the author of *Greece,
Rome, and the Bill of Rights* (1922) and *Public and
Private in Vergil's* Aeneid (1989), from which the following extract is taken. Here, Wiltshire addresses the
question of Vergil's attitude toward women as
expressed in the *Aeneid,* refuting claims that he is a
misogynist by noting that he considers private life
(dominated by women) to be as important as the public sphere.]

The schism between sexuality and competence in the public
realm in the *Aeneid* could lead to the conclusion that Vergil is a
virulent misogynist who rejects not only female but in fact all
sexuality. In such an argument, Vergil is seen to portray female

characters on both the human and the divine levels as irrational
and subordinate, while male characters are rational and hierar-
chically superior.

For example, Perkell hypothesizes that Vergil altered the traditional stories about Creusa and Dido expressly in order to
portray the women as victims of the Roman mission and
Aeneas's inattention. John P. Sullivan takes a similar position in
explaining Vergil's "latent misogyny," although he concedes
that it was partly conditioned by his cultural environment and
that it does not detract from his poetic genius.

In order to take into account how Vergil was limited by his
historical situation as well as how he saw beyond it, these
claims must be answered with a contradiction. They are both
false and true. On the one hand, it is not true that Vergil attrib-
utes irrationality solely to female characters. Turnus is capable
of acting irrationally, for example, and so is Aeneas. Vergil uses
the same word *amens,* "maddened, out of one's mind," for
Turnus at 7.460, *arma amens fremit,* and Aeneas at 2.314,
arma amens capio.

On the other hand, it is true that women in the *Aeneid* do
suffer disproportionately from the efforts required to found
Rome. It is true also that both divine and human females
behave irrationally in the epic. It would be bracing, even two
thousand years later, if order and disorder, rationality and irrationality, were always associated equally with both male and
female power. To wish such enlightened equity for the first century B.C.E., however, even for Vergil, is very much like Dante's
wishing Vergil could have been a Christian. It is simply
anachronistic.

That we do not see those things in an epic poem written two
millennia ago is not at all remarkable. The epic genre itself is
partly responsible for this; the heroic mode is not hospitable to
women. What is truly remarkable, and what makes him a femi-
nist in the broadest sense, is that in his poem Vergil takes the
private world as seriously as the public. It is extraordinary that
Vergil takes any account, much less the extensive account he
does, of the struggles, pains, hopes, and disappointments of
relationships in the private realm. The exquisite attention lav-

ished upon Dido, the eloquent lament of the mother of Euryalus, the grief of the sisters Anna and Juturna who cannot save the siblings they adore, the mourning of all the parents in the *Aeneid* who watch their children die young: Vergil's tribute to the victims is the measure of their worth. He could have written a polemic that treated these losses as unfortunate results of a necessary political program. Instead, he wrote a poem that memorialized the casualties. In his treatment of these subjects Vergil represents a futurity of consciousness about the values of the private, traditionally female world.

—Susan Ford Wiltshire, *Public and Private in Vergil's* Aeneid (Amherst: University of Massachusetts Press, 1989), pp. 119–21

❖

H.-P. Stahl on Aeneas and Augustus

[H.-P. Stahl is a professor of classics at the University of Pittsburgh. In this extract, Stahl examines the ways in which Aeneas can be compared to the emperor Augustus.]

In Vergil's version, Aeneas, ancestor of the Julian family, appears in Italy as a peaceful and peace-seeking newcomer. (Perhaps one should call him a homecomer since his distant forefather Dardanus had supposedly emigrated from here, *Aen.* 7.206f., 240; cf. 3.167.) His journey has been supervised by Fate and by Jupiter (1.261ff.; 8.381). He is sent under orders of Apollo, god of prophecy, specifically to occupy the land between Tiber and Numicus (7.241f.), i.e., territory held by King Latinus' people and by the Rutulians of King Turnus. The ultimate purpose of his arrival, according to divine revelation (7.98–101; cf. 1.286ff.), is the worldwide rule his descendant Augustus will one day peacefully exercise from around here.

Aeneas is not spared the saddening experience of resistance, raised by an increasing faction of the native population. There is, above all, oracle-defying, sacrilegious Turnus (cf. 7.595) who associates with such telltale characters as King Mezentius, most cruel torturer of his own subjects (8.485ff.) and "despiser of the gods" (*contemptor divum,* 8.7); another close companion of his is Messapus who, on the occasion of a peace treaty, delights in killing a king at the altar in full regalia as, in his words, "a better victim for the great gods" (12.289–96). The Julian ancestor is forced to wage a holy war against the godless opposition.

His greater descendant had to face comparable problems. After the assassination of his adoptive father, C. Julius Caesar (the dictator), Octavian (the later Augustus) joined the second triumvirate and its mandate "to organize the republic," *rei publicae constituendae.* Octavian wished his earthly achievements to be viewed as fulfillment of a divine mission—so much so that he would publicly spread the needed information. On a coin of his, one finds his public task, expressed by the three letters *r(ei) p(ublicae) c(onstituendae),* superimposed on the outline of a tripod, i.e., on the symbol of Apollo, god of prophecy, whom he considered his personal tutelary deity.

Octavian, as his *Achievements* inform posterity, had to defeat the men "who butchered my father" (*qui parentem meum trucidaverunt*—the customary label for a dictator's assassins, we remind ourselves, would be "tyrannicides"), "when they raised arms against the republic," *bellum inferentis rei publicae.* True to his perception of his mission as serving the common weal, he calls his opponents a "faction," not dignifying them by mentioning a name.

To sum up, then: a just cause; executor of a divine mission; administrator of the nation's interests; facing irresponsible, godless, and criminal factionalism—these are features shared by the founder of the Julian race (as depicted by Vergil) and by his descendant (as his case is presented by Augustus himself).

It was the ancestor's task, according to the *Aeneid,* to prepare the road that would, in the distant future (i.e., in Vergil's own time), lead to Emperor Augustus. Now: since the portrait of the forefather was being painted at a time (29–19 B.C.) when the descendant had already completed the conquest of his unholy opposition, one cannot a priori exclude that the epic on the ancestor may, at least in part, be designed to set the record "straight" on the ethics and metaphysics of the descendant's career. I do not want to state here "typological" correspondences between the two characters. Nor do I subscribe to the hypothesis that the poetic ancestor was intended to enlighten the real-life descendant about his obligations as a ruler. A question more to the point appears to be: could any reader in the time of Augustus fail to observe the symphonic pitch in epic and present-day political pronouncements, e.g., the declared desire for peace and the unwelcome burden of having had to wage a holy war against sacrilegious rebels who threatened the community? Is the ancestor's enduring loyalty to his divine mission not superbly helpful in guiding the reader and citizen when he ponders the presumed motivation of the latest Julian, his contemporary ruler (as well as that of his adversaries)?

—H.-P. Stahl, "The Death of Turnus: Augustan Vergil and the Political Rival," *Between Republic and Empire: Interpretations of Augustus and His Principate,* ed. Kurt A. Raaflaub and Mark Toher (Berkeley: University of California Press, 1990), pp. 174–76

❖

Marilynn Desmond on Dido

[Marilynn Desmond (b. 1952), a professor of English at the State University of New York at Binghamton, is the author of *Reading Dido* (1994), a study of the *Aeneid* and its influence in the mediaeval age from which the following extract is taken. Here, Desmond studies the figure of Dido, finding in her both a sexual and a political threat to Aeneas and Rome.]

Aeneid 4 juxtaposes erotic and political discourse in the narrative of Dido's disintegration and downfall; indeed, as Monti observes: "The emotional aspect of the Dido-Aeneas relationship does not obliterate its initial political character, but rather is an intensification and extension of it." Monti also notes that the speeches between Aeneas and Dido have a political quality. In the end, however, Dido's political role is compromised by her sexual behavior, and the destructive quality of her sexuality culminates in the phallic overtones of her death. Yet this suicide by sword is simultaneously a masculine death particularly appropriate to a tragic hero, so that Dido's death seems to cite Ajax's suicide in Sophocles' play.

Both Aeneas and Dido engage in the sexual activity that brings on disaster in *Aeneid* 4, but only Dido becomes tainted by *amor* and suffers a reversal of fortune. As Cairns's "kingship" paradigm suggests, Aeneas is tempered by his brush with sexual danger and leaves Carthage a better king while Dido and her city are destroyed. In her analysis of the politics of desire in Virgil's *Aeneid*, Mihoko Suzuki sees Dido as a character who embodies the "threat of the female Other." However, Dido's status as "Other" derives from the destabilizing effects of her erotic desires; in her public, political performance as "king" or leader, Dido—like her historical counterpart—does not figure difference. Virgil's bifurcated delineation of Dido's behavior as king and lover reflects Roman constructions of gender during the period of the consolidation of Roman colonial power under the structure of empire so that the female might become identified with the colonized other. As Judith Hallett has shown, the "elite Roman male conceptualization of the female sex is a bipartite one. One part appears to reflect an assumption of *sex polarity* and female alterity, a concept of woman as *Other* . . . the other part of this conceptualization, categorizing women as *Same*, reflects an assumption of *sex unity*, a view that unifies male and female by ascribing to the latter qualities and talents culturally valued in the former.

As a political leader, Dido exhibits the qualities that are valued in a heroic, male figure. As a woman who succumbs to erotic desire, Dido resembles another masculine stereotype, the "elegiac lover" in Cairns's analysis of the cultural allusions at work in *Aeneid* 4; the descriptions of Dido's role as a lover and her erotic symptoms of disease and sleeplessness conform closely to the elegiac stereotype of lovers. Virgil has transformed the historical Dido—a "good king" who is venerated as a deity after her death—into a literary figure explicitly defined by his or her difference from cultural norms; as Cairns comments, "the elegiac lover was weak, foolish, worthless and morally cuplable." Virgil has eroticized the historical figure of Dido, and in the process he has feminized erotic desire as it is conventionally expressed in elegy.

It is a commonplace of Virgil critcism that Dido represents two critical moments in the history of Roman colonization in her prediction of the Punic Wars and her figural identification with Cleopatra. Both Hannibal and Cleopatra had acquired mythic proportions as enemies who mounted a North African challenge to Roman dominance. Although described as one "fati nescia" (ignorant of fate), Dido has a prophetic moment in *Aeneid* 4 when her final curse on the departing Aeneas predicts Rome's wars with Carthage. Not only does she foretell the rise of Hannibal (4.625) when she prophesies an avenger in her name, she also provides an ideological interpretation for the geographical placement of Carthage and Rome in her assertion that the two peoples be forever "litora litoribus contraria" (4.628). Virgil's audience would recognize in this curse a proleptic view of Roman history: the fulfillment of the Roman ideal, prophesied in books 1, 6, and 8, would involve a long and bitter struggle with North Africa and the "brutal destruction of Carthage by Rome," as Steven Farron puts it.

In spite of the narrator's focus on her ignorance of fate, Dido's prophetic curse implicates her more directly in the telescopic sweep of Roman history than any of her other actions in *Aeneid* 4. Dido's identification with Carthage makes her a purposeful reminder that the narrative of Roman dominance in the Mediterranean was not a seamless myth of uncontested development and expansion: the centralization of colonial power depended on Roman ability to control and subjugate—if necessary—the territories at the periphery of the empire. Dido's status in the *Aeneid* allows us to consider the intersection of the discourses of gender and colonization at work in Augustan Rome and Virgil's text: Dido's colonial identity is emphasized by the fact that Virgil, in a departure from the historical tradition, connects Dido's death to the fall of Carthage, the rise of Hannibal, and eventually the subjugation of the city by the Romans. In Justin's account, by contrast, the city of Carthage survives the noble suicide of its queen.

Beyond her identification with Carthage, Dido also functions as a figure for Cleopatra; indeed, Roman perception of Cleopatra's role in the events culminating in the battle of Actium and the establishment of empire resonated powerfully with Dido's use of the phrase "litora litoribus contraria." Within the geopolitics of empire, Cleopatra's challenge was seen as a feminine, sexualized, oriental threat to centralized Roman power. As Ronald Syme has shown, Augustus worked to focus Italian attention not on his rival for supreme power Anthony—but on fears that Anthony intended to "subjugate Italy and the West under the rule of an Oriental queen." This particular vision of Actium is engraved on Aeneas's shield in *Aeneid* 8:

> hinc ope barbarica uariisque Antonius armis,
> uictor ab Aurorae populis et litore rubro,
> Aegyptum uirisque Orientis et ultima secum
> Bactra uehit, sequiturque (nefas) Aegyptia coniunx.   (8.685–88)

> On this side, with foreign wealth and diverse arms, Anthony, conqueror from the Red Sea and peoples of the East; he carries Egypt and the strength of the East and remote Bactra with him, and (horror!) an Egyptian consort follows.

The foundational discourse of Roman imperial power, particularly evident in the Augustan version of Actium visible here on Aeneas's shield, relies heavily on a depiction of the colonial enemy as a sexualized, racialized female other. In Dido, Hannibal and Cleopatra are eerily conflated to evoke an imperial vision of the enemy from the periphery who threatens centralized Roman power. In a discussion of Cleopatra, Lillian Robinson comments on the sexual politics of such gestures: "[Cleopatra's] oriental nature, always emphasized in Roman propaganda despite her Greek origin, implied unbridled sexuality." *Aeneid* 4 emphasizes Dido's sexuality, especially by contrast to Aeneas's dutiful behavior in his departure from Carthage in obedience to the gods.

Virgil's Dido represents a transformation of the "poetic memory" of the historical Dido in an orientalist gesture that displaces the erotic onto Dido as an African queen of Asian origin. *Aeneid* 4 specifically delineates the aspects of Dido's character that constitute a threat to Roman culture: it is Dido-as-lover (a Virgilian interpretation of the figure), not Dido-as-leader (the historical outlines of the figure), that embodies otherness and danger. Dido and Aeneas both have their origin in the East; yet Aeneas's story is that of a Trojan who becomes Italianized, while Dido's story suggests that she is, in the final analysis, incapable of suppressing her "oriental" nature. The Dido of *Aeneid* 1, whose "moenia surgunt" (437) is less a threat than the eroticized figure of *Aeneid* 4 whose "non coeptae adsurgunt turres" (86). It is not the female as sexual or female sexuality that occupies the position of otherness in the imperial politics of the *Aeneid*; rather, it is unconstrained sexuality itself that bears the mark of gender. Dido's role in the narrative of *Aeneid* 4 works to render sexuality in feminine terms. In the Roman ethnographic vision of the "oriental," the East is the locus of the dangerously sexual, and the dangerously sexual, when figured by Dido or Cleopatra, becomes feminized.

> —Marilynn Desmond, *Reading Dido: Gender, Textuality, and the Medieval* Aeneid (Minneapolis: University of Minnesota Press, 1994), pp. 30–33

❖

Michael C. J. Putnam on the Glory and Tragedy of Rome

[Michael C. J. Putnam, a professor of classics at Brown University, is the author of *The Poetry of the* Aeneid (1965), *Virgil's Pastoral Art: Studies in the* Eclogues (1970), *Virgil's Poem of the Earth: Studies in the* Georgics (1979) and other works. In this extract from his new study of the *Aeneid,* Putnam studies the death of Turnus at the end of the epic, showing how it embodies both the glory and the tragedy of Rome.]

Virgil proposes for Aeneas a passionate search for Roman identity when he is in fact an outsider—Trojan instead of *indiges,* allied with Jupiter instead of Italian Saturn, an overlord fated but foreign. Aeneas has no connection with the Roman penchant for identification with ancestors, for ordering through custom and rationalizing through law. We may grant him allegiance to Latinus' rich inheritance, to Evander's primeval ways, to Hercules' vindictive heroism, but by the end the very legality of his action is more open to question than acceptance. The emotional and intellectual ties with Pallas, *pietas* toward Arcadia, are poor balance for procreating the *persona* of Roman vengeance. The paradigm is Greek, not Roman, Homeric, not Stoic. Achilles rages at the death of Patroclus, but Pallas is no surrogate for Aeneas whose final deed smacks more of self-justification than humanism. The essential Roman dream, the habituation that makes peace practicable, the suppression of individual selfhood that makes clemency viable, is not allowed to enter Aeneas' mind.

Seen archetypally, Turnus' death is the (innocent) immolation whose bloodletting is vital to any foundation. Looked at against the background of Roman historical development, the killing of Turnus announces the end of the Roman Republic, of two orders balancing each other, of two consuls, of a popular tribune with veto power over aristocratic measures. Tacitus speaks of the time after the battle of Actium when *omnem potentiam ad unum conferri pacis interfuit* (*Histories* 1.1). What replaces liberty—and this is a chief significance of Turnus' loss—is peace, but a narrow peace, born of violence and founded on personal impulse and the ethics of revenge.

Frank Kermode, in his recent book *The Sense of an Ending*, speaks of the *Aeneid* (and Genesis) as an end-determined fiction. Unlike Odysseus' cyclic ritual, "the progress of Aeneas from the broken city of Troy to a Rome standing for empire without end, is closer to our traditional apocalyptic, and that is why his *imperium* has been incorporated into Western apocalyptic as a type of the City of God." We may see with justice the *Odyssey* as a journey, literal and symbolic, of departure and return and the *Aeneid* as an open-ended voyage of expansive intellectual and political accomplishment. But perhaps, too, the *Aeneid* in a very different way is a type of *Odyssey*, a cyclical evocation of emotion which transcends the temporal propulsion of history. It is true that Troy leads to Rome, loss to fulfillment of a sort, tragedy to a type of comedy, and there is one whole level of intent—an idealistic level of fated prophecies, divine inspirations, and somniac revelations—where the mastery of a perfected Rome is acclaimed. But in the poetry of action, where deed challenges word and the poet's involvement runs most deeply, mortal means obscure and corrupt apocalyptic ends. And on this level the *Aeneid* is a cycle both revelatory and humane, leading from pain and wrath on the divine level ultimately to the same emotions reconstructed by the quasi-divinized hero. The *Aeneid* is a very Roman poem not so much because it presents a vision of *imperium* functioning with civilized, and civilizing, grandeur or because it predisposes us toward a higher Stoic morality than that which a Homeric hero might contemplate (and in so doing be said to anticipate Augustine's *City* and Dante's *Paradiso*). The cycle of Roman *Aeneid*, which begins in Troy and ends with Homer, is internal and metaphysical, a cycle of madness at its conclusion appraising the primal Roman myth of two brothers who do violence to each other and of the loss of liberty than any resulting triumph or defeat portends. Peace at times means suppression, as the greatest Latin historians warn. This cycle of rage reflects Rome's past and, as Virgil would have well known, mankind's future. Eternal, boundless Rome is mortal, after all.

In spite of the "mythical" setting of the *Aeneid*, there is a gradual hardening and toughening of Virgil's version of reality as his work progresses. In the *Eclogues* the outside world is only vaguely imagined by even the shepherds who most suffer its inroads. By manufacturing miraculous vistas of the future or dwelling on poetry per se, it is easy enough to escape life's more inimical pressures. In the *Georgics* Virgil faces the beauties and hardships of life with the soil, but first by metaphor and then by myth extends his ambivalent insights to the world of men. At the end we are left to ask what can reconcile the leisured poet-singer with conquering Octavian. But it is the combined tales of Aristaeus and Orpheus which both summarize and forecast the outcome of the *Aeneid*. If a bard gifted with magic sufficient to tame the Underworld and evoke the dead to life cannot restrain his mortal *furor*, what of those with lesser gifts but more power? What in fact of those like thundering Octavian whose profession by nature could all too easily lend itself to violence? In spite of the accomplishments of the *pax Augusta,* the *Aeneid* warns of the suffering and terror in the establishment and maintenance of an empire still challengingly remote in the *Eclogues.* Through the medium of myth, movement back in time ironically brings us closer to essential matters, to prospective growth and stability but also to suffering, exile, and the final exile, death. It is this realistic appraisal of Rome and of life's ultimate ambivalence—the glory but also finally the tragedy—that at the present time continues to earn for the *Aeneid* its status as a masterpiece.

—Michael C. J. Putnam, *Virgil's* Aeneid: *Interpretation and Influence* (Chapel Hill: University of North Carolina Press, 1995), pp. 24–26

❖

Books by Vergil

Latin text:

Opera. 1470.

[*Works.*] Ed. Nicolaas Heinsius. 1649.

Opera. Ed. Otto Ribbeck. 1859–68. 5 vols.

Works. Ed. John Conington. 1858–71 (3 vols.); rev. (with Henry Nettleship) 1871–75 (3 vols.).

Opera. Ed. Sir Frederic Arthur Hirtzel. 1900.

[*Works.*] Ed. Henri Goelzer and René Durand. 1925–36. 4 vols.

Opera. Ed. Walther Janell. 1930.

Tutte le opere. Ed. Enzio Cetrangolo. 1966.

Opera. Ed. R. A. B. Mynors. 1969.

Aeneid. Ed. R. D. Williams. 1972–73. 2 vols.

English translations:

The XII. Bukes of Eneados of the Famose Poete Virgill. Tr. Gawin Douglas. 1553.

Certain Bokes of Virgiles Aenaeis. Tr. Henry Howard, Earl of Surrey. 1557.

[*Aeneid.*] Tr. Thomas Phaer and Thomas Twyne. 1573.

Bucoliks. Tr. Abraham Fleming. 1589.

Works. Tr. John Ogilby. 1649.

Works. Tr. John Dryden. 1697.

Works. Tr. Joseph Davidson. 1847.

[*Works.*] Tr. John Conington. 1872 (in Conington's *Miscellaneous Writings*, Vol. 2).

Aeneid. Tr. William Morris. 1876.

Aeneid. Tr. J. W. Mackail. 1885.

Eclogues and Georgics. Tr. J. W. Mackail. 1889.

Aeneid. Tr. James Rhoades. 1893–96. 2 vols.

Aeneid. Tr. Arthur S. Way. 1916–30. 4 vols.

The Poems of Virgil. Tr. James Rhoades. 1921.

Georgics. Tr. C. Day Lewis. 1940.

Aeneid. Tr. Rolfe Humphries. 1951.

Aeneid. Tr. C. Day Lewis. 1952.

Aeneid. Tr. W. F. Jackson Knight. 1956.

Eclogues. Tr. C. Day Lewis. 1963.

Aeneid. Tr. Allen Mandelbaum. 1971.

Aeneid. Tr. Robert Fitzgerald. 1983.

Works about
Vergil and the *Aeneid*

Anderson, W. S. *The Art of the* Aeneid. Englewood Cliffs, NJ: Prentice-Hall, 1969.

Arethusa 14, No. 1 (Spring 1981). Special Vergil issue.

Bernard, John D., ed. *Vergil at 2000.* New York: AMS Press, 1986.

Bloom, Harold, ed. *Virgil.* New York: Chelsea House, 1986.

Boyle, A. J. *The Chaonian Dove: Studies in the* Eclogues, Georgics *and* Aeneid. *Mnemosyne* Suppl. 95. Leiden: E. J. Brill, 1986.

Camps, W. A. *An Introduction to Virgil's* Aeneid. Oxford: Oxford University Press, 1969.

Clark, Raymond J. *Catabasis: Vergil and the Wisdom-Tradition.* Amsterdam: Gruner, 1979.

Clausen, Wendell. *Virgil's* Aeneid *and the Tradition of Hellenistic Poetry.* Berkeley: University of California Press, 1987.

Commager, Steele, ed. *Virgil: A Collection of Critical Essays.* Englewood Cliffs, NJ: Prentice-Hall, 1966.

Conte, Gian Biagio. *The Rhetoric of Imitation: Genre and Poetic Memory in Virgil and Other Latin Poets.* Ithaca, NY: Cornell University Press, 1986.

Di Cesare, Mario A. *The Altar and the City: A Reading of Virgil's* Aeneid. New York: Columbia University Press, 1974.

Distler, Paul F. *Vergil and Vergiliana.* Chicago: Loyola University Press, 1966.

Drew, Douglas Laurel. *The Allegory of the* Aeneid. New York: Garland, 1978.

Dudley, D. R., ed. *Virgil.* London: Routledge & Kegan Paul, 1969.

Farron, Steven. *Vergil's* Aeneid: *A Poem of Grief and Love.* Leiden: E. J. Brill, 1993.

Feeney, D. C. *The Gods in Epic: Poets and Critics of the Classical Tradition.* Oxford: Clarendon Press, 1991.

Galinsky, G. Karl. "The Anger of Aeneas." *American Journal of Philology* 109 (1988): 321–48.

Gillis, Daniel. *Eros and Death in the* Aeneid. Rome: L'Erma di Bretschneider, 1983.

Glover, T. R. *Virgil.* 4th ed. London: Methuen, 1920.

Gransden, K. W. *Virgil's* Aeneid: *An Essay on Epic Narrative.* Cambridge: Cambridge University Press, 1984.

Hardie, Philip R. *Virgil's* Aeneid: *Cosmos and Imperium.* Oxford: Clarendon Press, 1986.

Harrison, E. L. "The *Aeneid* and Carthage." In *Poetry and Politics in the Age of Augustus,* ed. Tony Woodman and David West. Cambridge: Cambridge University Press, 1984, pp. 95–115.

Harrison, S. J., ed. *Oxford Readings in Vergil's* Aeneid. Oxford: Clarendon Press, 1990.

Highet, Gilbert. *The Speeches in Vergil's* Aeneid. Princeton: Princeton University Press, 1972.

Jackson Knight, W. F. *Roman Virgil.* 2nd ed. London: Faber & Faber, 1966.

Lee, M. Owen. *Fathers and Sons in Virgil's* Aeneid: *Tum Genitor Natum.* Albany: State University of New York Press, 1979.

Lyne, R. O. A. M. *Further Voices in Vergil's* Aeneid. Oxford: Clarendon Press, 1986.

Mack, Sara. *Patterns of Time in Virgil.* Hamden, CT: Archon, 1978.

Montagu, John R. C., ed. *Cicero and Virgil: Studies in Honour of Harold Hunt.* Amsterdam: Adolf M. Hakkert, 1972.

Moskalew, Walter. *Formular Language and Poetic Design in the* Aeneid. *Mnemosyne* Suppl. 73. Leiden: E. J. Brill, 1982.

O'Hara, James. *Death and the Optimistic Prophecy in Vergil's* Aeneid. Princeton: Princeton University Press, 1990.

Otis, Brooks. "Virgilian Narrative in the Light of Its Precursors and Successors." *Studies in Philology* 73 (1976): 1–28.

Pavlock, Barbara. "Epic and Tragedy in Vergil's Nisus and Euryalus Episode." *Transactions of the American Philological Association* 115 (1985): 207–24.

Putnam, Michael C. J. "*Aeneid* VII and the *Aeneid*." *American Journal of Philology* 91 (1970): 408–30.

————. *The Poetry of the* Aeneid. Cambridge: Harvard University Press, 1965.

Quinn, Kenneth. *Virgil's* Aeneid: *A Critical Description.* Ann Arbor: University of Michigan Press, 1968.

Segal, C. P. "Art and the Hero: Participation, Detachment and Narrative Point of View in *Aeneid* 1." *Arethusa* 14 (1981): 67–83.

Slavitt, David R. *Virgil.* New Haven: Yale University Press, 1991.

Thornton, Agathe. *The Living Universe: Gods and Men in Virgil's* Aeneid. *Mnemosyne* Suppl. 46. Leiden: E. J. Brill, 1976.

Van Nortwick, T. "Aeneas, Turnus and Achilles." *Transactions of the American Philological Association* 110 (1980): 303–14.

Wilhelm, Robert M., and Howard Jones, eds. *The Two Worlds of the Poet: New Perspectives on Vergil.* Detroit: Wayne State University Press, 1992.

Willcock, M. M. "Battle Scenes in the *Aeneid*." *Proceedings of the Cambridge Philological Society* 29 (1983): 87–99.

Williams, Gordon. *Change and Decline: Roman Literature in the Early Empire.* Berkeley: University of California Press, 1978.

————. *Tradition and Originality in Roman Poetry.* Oxford: Clarendon Press, 1968.

Williams, R. D., and T. S. Pattie. *Virgil: His Poetry through the Ages.* London: British Library, 1982.

Wilson, C. H. "Jupiter and the Fates in the *Aeneid*." *Classical Quarterly* 29 (1979): 361–71.

Index of Themes and Ideas